X24

Contents

Getting the Most from Your KitchenAid® Stand Mixer

You count on your KitchenAid stand mixer to mix cookies, whip egg whites and knead bread dough, but there are countless other ways it can make cooking and baking easier, better and more enjoyable. Every stand mixer comes with three basic attachments: the flat beater, wire whip and dough hook. Here are some tips on making the best use of all three.

 ## Flat Beater

The flat beater is probably the attachment you use most. It's perfect for creaming butter and sugar, combining ingredients, beating cake batters and many other basic tasks. Use  it for: cakes, creamed frostings, candies, cookies, pie pastry, biscuits, quick breads, meat loaf and mashed potatoes.

SPEED TO SPARE

Your KitchenAid stand mixer will mix faster and more thoroughly than most other mixers. When converting traditional recipes, bear in mind that times must be adjusted to avoid overbeating. With cakes from scratch, for example, beating time may be half as long as with other mixers. (For more on converting recipes, see your KitchenAid stand mixer instruction and recipe book.)

Cutting Butter or Shortening into Flour

Your KitchenAid stand mixer makes short work of short doughs, including biscuits, pie pastry and scones without overworking the dough. Cut chilled butter or shortening into pieces and add it to the flour in the mixer bowl. Turn the flat beater to low and mix until the mixture resembles coarse crumbs (or the texture specified for a particular recipe). You'll keep your hands clean and the butter cold, which makes for a lighter and flakier result.

 ## Wire Whip

The wire whip is the attachment to reach for when air needs to be incorporated into a mixture. This includes recipes that call for beaten egg whites, like soufflés, angel food cakes, sponge  cakes and French macarons. The whip is also perfect for making mayonnaise or boiled frostings and, of course, for whipping cream.

How to Whip Egg Whites

It's easiest to separate egg yolks from whites when the eggs are cold, however, room temperature whites achieve greater volume. Be careful to keep all of the yolk, or any other fat, out of the egg whites. A drop or two of yolk is enough to prevent proper whipping.

Place the room temperature whites in a clean, dry mixer bowl. (Even a tiny bit of leftover grease in the bowl could prevent the whites from achieving volume.) Attach the wire whip. Whip, gradually increasing the speed to high. Beat until the egg whites reach the desired stage.

Foamy or Frothy: Large uneven air bubbles form.

Soft Peaks: Whites form a peak when lifted, but tips fall over when the whip is removed.

Stiff, Shiny Peaks: Sharp stiff peaks remain even when the whip is removed. Egg whites are glossy.

Sweetened Whipped Cream

- 1½ **cups heavy cream**
- ¼ **cup powdered sugar**
- ½ **teaspoon vanilla**

Place mixer bowl and wire whip in the freezer for 15 minutes to chill. Attach wire whip; pour cold heavy cream into mixer bowl. To avoid splashing, begin whipping on low and gradually increase speed to high. When cream forms soft peaks, add powdered sugar and vanilla and continue beating until the desired consistency. (Do not overbeat or cream will become grainy.)

MAKES ABOUT 3 CUPS. MAY BE DOUBLED.

A CRASH COURSE IN CREAM

Labels on containers of cream can be mystifying. Here are some definitions.

Light Cream (18 to 30% butterfat): Generally the same as half-and-half. Will only whip if it contains 30% butterfat.

Whipping Cream (30% butterfat): Will whip and thicken, but not as well as heavy cream.

Heavy Whipping Cream (36 to 38% butterfat): Whips up well and holds its shape. Doubles in volume when whipped.

Pasteurized vs. Ultra-Pasteurized: Ultra-pasteurized whipping cream has been heated to a higher temperature than regular pasteurized cream in order to extend its shelf life. Ultra-pasteurized cream takes longer to whip and will not retain peaks like pasteurized cream.

WHAT IS CREAM OF TARTAR ANYWAY?

Adding an acid ingredient to egg whites helps keep the foam more stable once it's whipped. Cream of tartar is usually the suggested acid, although lemon juice or even vinegar will work. And no, cream of tartar is not a milk product or what the dentist removes when he cleans your teeth. It's sediment produced on barrels during wine making. It is also the acidic ingredient in many baking powders.

Dough Hook

The dough hook is a breadmaker's best friend. Use it for mixing and kneading yeast doughs including breads, rolls, coffee cakes and buns.

What You Knead to Know

Yeast is alive. Use a kitchen thermometer to check liquids. Temperatures that are too high can kill the yeast and low temperatures will slow yeast growth and the time required for bread to rise.

Most bread recipes call for a range in the amount of flour. You'll know you've added enough when dough clings to the hook and cleans the side of the bowl. Some dough, especially when made with whole grains, may not form a ball on the hook. As long as the hook is making contact with the dough, it is being kneaded. Always keep the speed low while using the dough hook. Refer to the stand mixer instruction book for details.

Rising times vary due to any number of factors, including the temperature and humidity level in your kitchen. To judge whether dough has doubled, press into it lightly with your fingers. If the indentations remain, the dough has risen enough.

Fresh Pasta the Easy Way

Pasta Sheet Roller and Cutters

You'll find more information, suggested roller settings and basic recipes on pages 79 through 81. Even with the same recipe, pasta dough seems to change every time you make it. It can behave differently depending on the size of the eggs, brand of flour and even the temperature and humidity in the room. Preparation instructions are included with the recipes, but here are some troubleshooting tips.

Dough Gets Crumbly When Put Through the Rollers.

Don't worry if your dough shreds a bit the first time it's fed through thickness setting 1. The Pasta Sheet Roller will help smooth it out. Fold the dough in thirds and keep rolling and feeding it through the rollers at setting 1 at least three times. Continue until it becomes smooth and pliable before moving to the next setting.

There is something very satisfying about creating a delicious dinner from not much more than humble flour and eggs. Dried packaged pasta is convenient and tasty, but it just can't compare with the flavor and texture of fresh pasta you make yourself. With KitchenAid attachments, pasta making is fun and virtually foolproof. There's no laborious kneading or tricky rolling. Invite the kids or friends to help and pasta making may be as much fun as pasta eating. Once you've mastered basic egg pasta, try fettuccine made from whole wheat or use the Pasta Sheet Roller to enclose basil leaves in your dough. The pasta possibilities are endless!

> **SEMOLINA FLOUR**
>
> Semolina flour is made from durum wheat. Durum is a hard wheat (high in protein) that is used for commercial dried pasta. Adding semolina flour to your pasta dough makes a bit firmer noodle. Be careful when purchasing semolina, however, since grain labeled just "semolina" can be a coarser grind used for porridge like farina. You need finely ground semolina flour. It's available in large supermarkets, Italian markets and online.

Dough Sticks to the Rollers.

Sprinkle flour on the piece of dough before you feed it through the rollers and on the work surface as well. Don't rush through the roller settings. Remember that setting 1 is helping to knead the dough, so keep flouring and feeding it through until it is pliable, but not sticky. (Also make sure you are at setting 1 and not at a higher, thinner setting by mistake.) Clean the rollers with a brush to remove any stuck-on dough between batches.

Dough Is Sticky and Hard to Handle.

Don't forget to let the dough rest for at least 20 minutes and up to an hour at room temperature before rolling. This gives the gluten (the stretchy protein in flour) a chance to develop and gives flour time to thoroughly absorb liquid. If you can't finish making the pasta right away, store well-wrapped dough in the refrigerator for up to three days. Let it return to room temperature before rolling.

Noodles Stick Together after Being Cut.

It helps to gently separate noodles with floured fingers as they exit the cutting blades. Fan them out on a floured kitchen towel or sheet of parchment paper. Pasta should be dried for 10 minutes before cooking it. You can hang long pasta on a pasta drying rack or over a clean towel on the back of a chair or cabinet door. If you have the space, pasta can also be draped over a clean

sheet spread over a counter or table. You can even improvise a pasta rack with clean coat hangers.

Pasta Breaks into Short Pieces Instead of Long Noodles.

If you are working with whole wheat or spinach pasta, it's best to choose fettuccine or another fairly wide cutter. Because of the fiber in the dough, these pastas don't cut cleanly into narrow noodles like angel hair. It's also possible that you've let the pasta sheets dry for too long and they've become brittle. Fortunately, even pasta that looks less than perfect still tastes very good!

STORING HOMEMADE PASTA

Once it is dry, pasta can be stored in a plastic bag or airtight container in the refrigerator where it will keep for up to three days. For longer storage, freeze pasta for up to four months. Arrange pasta on a floured piece of parchment paper on a baking sheet. To handle long pasta shapes, flour the noodles and arrange them into round nests to save space and provide convenient portions. Freeze pasta for a day until solid and then transfer it to a freezer bag or other freezer container. There's no need to defrost pasta before cooking. Just add it to boiling water and cook for a bit longer than you would for fresh.

dough should be as wide as the rollers and rolled to thickness setting 4. Thinner dough sheets can break and leak filling. Narrower sheets won't fill properly. Let dough sheets dry on a flat surface for 10 minutes before making ravioli.

PRACTICE MAKES PERFECT RAVIOLI

The first time you use your ravioli maker, try feeding a pasta sheet through the rollers without adding filling to get a feel for things. And don't despair if your first sheet of real ravioli comes out lopsided or has partial raviolis at the edge. You'll soon master the exact quantities of filling and turns of the handle needed.

Troubleshooting Tips

Pasta sheets need to be uniformly wide and thick to feed into the machine evenly. Trim the edges of dough if necessary beforehand and flour the sheets as needed to prevent sticking. Be careful not to add filling too quickly (usually one scoop of filling at a time with the provided spoon is enough) since it can prevent raviolis from sealing properly. Spinach or nut fillings need to be smooth purees for the same reason. Make sure all of the filling is enclosed before the end of the pasta sheet or you risk getting filling on the rollers.

Let the finished ravioli sheets dry on a lightly floured surface for 10 minutes before separating them, one by one, along the perforations. Let them dry or freeze them in a single layer to prevent sticking. Before beginning a new sheet of ravioli, brush away any dried dough from the last batch and dust the rollers with flour.

Ravioli Maker

Turn out dozens of picture perfect ravioli in a matter of minutes with the KitchenAid® Ravioli Maker. It fills prepared sheets of pasta and even crimps the edges. Consult the instruction book for detailed directions on using this attachment. For a ravioli dough recipe, see page 89.

Preparing the Dough Sheets.

To feed correctly through the Ravioli Maker, dough sheets should be ⅟₁₆ of an inch thick and 5½ inches wide. Using the Pasta Sheet Roller, this means that

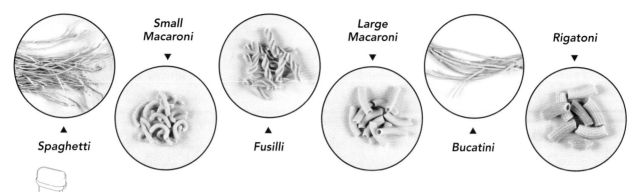

Small Macaroni ▼

▲ *Spaghetti*

Fusilli ▲

Large Macaroni ▼

Bucatini ▲

Rigatoni ▼

Pasta Press

Now homemade rigatoni is within reach! The KitchenAid® Pasta Press attachment lets you choose from six pasta shapes. It's fast and easy. Simply attach the desired pasta plate, feed dough into the hopper and press out macaroni, fusilli, spaghetti, rigatoni and even bucatini. (Read the instruction book that comes with your Pasta Press carefully for assembly, cleaning and safety instructions.)

Because the Pasta Press extrudes dough through a die, the texture of the dough is a bit different than from dough used with the Pasta Roller and Cutter attachments. It needs to be drier and more like pie crust or biscuit dough. Recipes for Eggless Pasta Dough as well as Whole Wheat Dough for the Pasta Press are on page 81.

Helpful Tips

The dough should be fed gradually into the hopper in walnut-sized pieces. Add additional dough after the previous pieces have disappeared into the hopper. If the first few noodles come out broken or ragged, squeeze the dough back together and return it to the hopper.

Keep the wire cutter clean of dried dough. Separate long pasta pieces gently with floured hands as they come out of the press so they don't stick together. Arrange short pasta in a single layer on a lightly floured sheet of parchment or a clean kitchen towel. Hang longer pasta from a drying rack and keep it separated. Consult the instruction book for the different extrusion speeds required for different pasta shapes.

COOKING PERFECT FRESH PASTA

Bringing a big pot of water to a boil to cook pasta takes time, so don't leave it to the last minute. Salting the water is not required, but can be important for flavor, especially if there is no salt in the pasta recipe itself. How much salt? There are as many answers to that question as there are Italian grandmas. For 6 quarts of water you'll need at least a few tablespoons. Add the pasta only after the water is at a full boil. Stir gently to keep the noodles from sticking together. Once the water returns to a boil, watch closely. Thin pasta can be done in one minute while thicker cuts may take five to seven minutes. The best way to know pasta is al dente and done to your liking is to remove a piece and taste it. Remember, too, that residual heat will continue cooking the pasta a bit while it drains. It's better to err on the side of slightly undercooked.

Ice Cream Made Simple

With the KitchenAid® Ice Cream Maker attachment you can create classic creamy chocolate and vanilla ice creams, custom flavors, gelatos, sorbets and more. Mix in your favorite candy, fruit or nuts. Experiment with savory flavors or exotic fruits. Try Cinnamon Honey Ice Cream on page 166, or Espresso Gelato on page 178. There's a world of choices beyond chocolate and vanilla!

The Cold, Cold Facts

There's one important rule for making ice cream—everything must be very cold. Keep the ice cream bowl and dasher in the freezer for AT LEAST 15 hours before using it. In fact, the best way to be ready is to always store the bowl in the freezer between batches. Don't remove it until everything is set to go and your ice cream mixture is cold, too.

You can chill your ice cream mixture by refrigerating it until cold (40°F), which will take at least two hours. If you don't want to wait (and who wants to wait for ice cream?) make an ice water bath. Nestle the prepared bowl of ice cream mixture inside a larger bowl of ice water. Let it stand for about one hour stirring occasionally, and adding ice to the bigger bowl if needed, until the mixture reaches 40°F.

> **RIPENING ICE CREAM**
>
> It's an odd word, but ripening is the term used for freezing freshly churned ice cream until firm. The consistency of just-churned ice cream is about that of soft-serve, but after an hour or two in the freezer it becomes firm enough to scoop.

Turning and Churning

It is extremely important to assemble the frozen bowl and dasher and turn your mixer on before pouring in the cold ice cream mixture. If you add it to the bowl before the dasher is turning, it can freeze immediately and cause the dasher to slip.

Always set your mixer to the lowest stir speed. Generally ice cream is ready after 20 to 25 minutes of churning, when it has reached the consistency of soft-serve ice cream. Timing does vary somewhat depending on ingredients. If the dasher begins to slip and make a clicking noise, the ice cream is done.

When mixing in solid ingredients, like candy, chocolate chips, fruit or nuts, wait until the final two minutes of the mixing process to add them.

Turn Up the Volume

Your KitchenAid® Ice Cream Maker has a larger bowl than many other machines. The yield for most recipes is 8 cups or 2 quarts. Be aware that ice cream increases in volume substantially as it churns. Never overfill the bowl or start with more than 46 ounces of liquid.

> **THE SCOOP ON SCOOPING**
>
> Once your ice cream is thoroughly frozen (ripened) it may be too solid to scoop right out of the freezer. Allow it to sit at room temperature for 5 to 10 minutes or help things along by microwaving it for 20 to 30 seconds on low power. Running your ice cream scoop under hot water first also helps.

Put the Rotor Slicer/Shredder to Work on Anything from Soup to Nuts

Need to slice onions for Oven-Roasted Onion Soup (page 104)? Shred cabbage for Okonomiyaki (page 58)? Slice veggies for chips? The Rotor Slicer/ Shredder attachment just may be the most versatile tool you can use with your stand mixer. Choose the appropriate cone for the job and make quick work of what used to be tedious chores.

Always follow assembly and safety directions in the KitchenAid® Rotor Slicer/Shredder instruction book that comes with the attachment.

Which Cone for What Job?

Cones are numbered on their closed ends.

Fine Shredder (cone number 1): Use this to finely shred hard, crisp vegetables, including carrots, beets, turnips, potatoes and celery. Also good for shredding firm cold cheese, coconut and dried bread.

Coarse Shredder (cone number 2): Use this to coarsely shred carrots, celery or onions and to make coarse shredded potatoes for potato pancakes. Also shreds some fruits, nuts and chocolate.

Thick Slicer (cone number 3): Use this to thickly slice firm vegetables that are to be steamed, fried, scalloped or creamed.

Thin Slicer (cone number 4): Use this to get thin slices of vegetables for slaw, potato chips, sauerkraut, pickles and salads.

CLEAN UP TIPS

The Rotor Slicer/Shredder housing and cones are dishwasher safe. Some foods, such as carrots, may stain the housing. Remove stubborn stains by rubbing a small amount of oil over them, washing in warm sudsy water and rinsing thoroughly.

Helpful Tips

Shredding cheeses, especially soft ones like Gouda or Monterey Jack, is easier if they are very cold or even partially frozen. Place them in the freezer for 20 minutes before shredding.

Vegetables should be cut into sizes that fit in the hopper. You can use half of the hopper for narrow items like carrots by lifting the handle on just one side. If you wish to make round slices, stand the vegetable up vertically in the hopper. Remember, you can change cone sizes to handle multiple tasks without disassembling the housing.

WHY BOTHER TO SHRED CHEESE?

Packs of shredded cheese are readily available, so why take the time to shred it at home? The most obvious reason is that it's considerably more economical. Check prices on a one pound block of Cheddar versus one pound of shredded Cheddar (4 cups). Choices of packaged shredded cheese are also limited to the mainstream varieties— no Gouda or Fontina. And did you know that shredded cheese contains anticaking agents? They usually include potato starch and powdered cellulose.

Grind Big Jobs Down to Size with the KitchenAid® Food Grinder

No wonder the Food Grinder is one of the best selling attachments for the stand mixer: It makes quick work of burgers, falafel, sausage, pesto, salsa and much more.

Two different plates—coarse and fine—let you control the texture. The coarse plate can be used for grinding raw or cooked meats, firm vegetables, dried fruit and cheese. Use the fine plate for finer textured raw meat, cooked meat for spreads or for making bread crumbs. Food should be cut into pieces or strips that easily fit into the hopper. Always use the food pusher to feed food into the hopper.

Most salsas and relishes can be made by grinding ingredients together—no need to chop parsley or cilantro or mince garlic beforehand. Just add sprigs of herbs or peeled cloves of garlic to the hopper. The Food Grinder can handle wedges of onion or tomatillos, too. Pesto sauce made with the grinder has a slightly coarser texture than when

it's made in a blender, more like real Italian pesto made with a mortar and pestle. See the instruction booklet for more recipe ideas as well as assembly instructions and safety precautions.

Meat Matters

With the Food Grinder, you can turn humble beef chuck into the Ultimate Grilled Burger (page 86) or make homemade breakfast sausage with your own signature spice blend. Grinding at home lets you decide on the kind, quality and cut of meat that goes into the finished product. No worries about extenders, additives or other mystery ingredients. You control the amount of fat and know exactly when it was ground. (Who knows how long supermarket ground meat has been sitting shrink-wrapped in its plastic tray.) Need more reasons? Freshly ground meat tastes better and grinding your own can save you money.

BUT WHAT'S PORK BUTT?

It's not what it sounds like! Pork butt, which is also called Boston butt, is actually pork shoulder and an excellent cut to use for sausage. It's called butt because a century or so ago, pork shoulder roasts were packed and shipped, often from Boston, in a barrel called a butt.

Maple Sage Breakfast Sausage

3 **pounds boneless pork shoulder (butt), cut into 2-inch strips**

⅓ **cup real maple syrup (not pancake syrup)**

1 **tablespoon kosher salt**

1 **tablespoon chopped fresh sage**

1 **teaspoon dried thyme**

1 **teaspoon red pepper flakes**

1 **teaspoon freshly ground black pepper**

½ **teaspoon freshly grated nutmeg**

1 Spread pork on baking sheet. Refrigerate or freeze until slightly firm.

2 Assemble Food Grinder with coarse grinding plate. Grind pork into mixing bowl. Add remaining ingredients to mixing bowl. Replace Food Grinder with flat beater. Mix 1 minute or until well blended.

3 Shape mixture into 3-inch patties. Heat large skillet over medium heat; cook patties 3 minutes per side until browned and cooked through (160°F).

MAKES 8 TO 10 SERVINGS

Tips for Smooth Grinding

Keep things cold. The easiest grinding and best texture result when meat is very cold or even partially frozen. After cutting meat into strips that will fit into the hopper of the Food Grinder, spread them in a single layer on a parchment- or foil-lined baking sheet. Refrigerate or freeze until firm. This will take 20 to 30 minutes in the refrigerator or about 15 minutes in the freezer. It's fine to use cheaper, tougher cuts of meat for sausage making. Shoulder cuts, like pork butt or beef chuck are preferred since they result in flavorful, juicy sausage. Trim any gristle or connective tissue as you cut the meat into strips.

Fat facts. Sausage needs some fat for flavor, but your homemade sausage will contain considerably less than almost any prepared product. Fresh pork fatback is usually recommended since it has a mild flavor and good texture. The term "fatback" refers to the layer of white fat that runs along a hog's back. Most butchers will be happy to sell you fatback at a reasonable price. Don't confuse fresh pork fatback with cured or smoked pork belly or salt pork, which are used for other kinds of recipes.

Be patient. Don't try to hurry the process by stuffing too much meat into the hopper or pressing down too hard on the pusher. Slow and steady keeps the meat cold and prevents the ground meat from becoming mushy or jamming the machine. Always return the seasoned ground meat to the refrigerator right after mixing it.

Links versus patties. Once ground, sausage can be formed into patties or stuffed into casings to make links. Most sausage recipes, including the ones in this book, are delicious either way. But once you experience the fun of sausage making, you'll probably want to turn it into professional looking links that are ready for the grill. With the help of the KitchenAid® Sausage Stuffer attachment for your Food Grinder, it's a lot easier than you might think.

Conquering casings. Purchasing and using sausage casings is actually fairly straightforward. Natural hog casings in a medium size are the most common since they are easy to work with and readily available. Relax! They come already cleaned and are usually packed in salt. You only have to rinse and soak the casings before use to remove the salt. Your butcher will probably sell you natural casings if you ask, or you can easily order them online. One pound of meat will use about 2 feet of casings. Unused salted casings can be refrigerated for up to a year. Vegetarian and collagen casings are also available, though a bit more difficult to work with.

Consult the Sausage Stuffer instruction book for directions on handling casings, filling sausages and forming links.

Sauces and Purees the Easy Way

The KitchenAid® Fruit/Vegetable Strainer works with the Food Grinder to turn out silky applesauce, healthy homemade baby food, perfect raspberry coulis and much more. It purees any soft fruit or cooked vegetable and gets rid of seeds and skins. And it does all the work without straining your arm or staining your strainer!

Before processing fruits with tough thick skin (like oranges or grapefruits) remove the skin; also remove any large pits (like peach pits). Hulls and stems (including strawberry hulls and tomato stems) must also be removed. Vegetables and firm fruits must be cooked before processing.

If liquid collects in the hopper while you are straining high moisture foods such as tomatoes, do not add additional food. Keep the mixer

---

USE GRAPE CAUTION!

Slip-skin type grapes (the Labruscan family), including Concords, Catawba and Ontario grapes should NOT be processed in the Fruit/Vegetable Strainer. Damage to the attachment or the mixer could result. Only grapes from the Ninifera family, including Tokay and Thompson seedless may be processed.

---

running until residual moisture drains. Consult the instruction book for details.

Prepare for Pulp

In addition to placing the mixing bowl under the spout to catch pureed fruit or juice, you'll need another bowl to catch the pulp that comes out of the center of the strainer housing. You can adjust the texture of the finished product with this pulp. For Raspberry Coulis, put the collected pulp back in the hopper and strain again. Discard the remaining pulp, which will consist mostly of raspberry seeds. For perfectly smooth baby food or applesauce, discard all the collected pulp.

The Food Tray: Extra Room for Big Jobs

When you're putting up a summer's worth of tomatoes from the garden, add the Food Tray to the Fruit/Vegetable Strainer. It fits over the hopper of the Food Grinder so you spend less time reloading. It can also be used with the Food Grinder and Sausage Stuffer and is helpful when grinding large quantities of meat or stuffing sausages.

Raspberry Coulis

3 cups fresh raspberries

1 tablespoon sugar (or more depending on sweetness of fruit)

2 teaspoons lemon juice

Assemble Food Grinder with Fruit/Vegetable Strainer and attach to stand mixer. Feed raspberries into hopper and collect raspberry purée in mixer bowl. Collect pulp in another bowl. Return pulp to hopper and strain again into mixer bowl. Stir in sugar and lemon juice until dissolved. Discard remaining pulp.

Make the Citrus Juicer Your Main Squeeze

Got a lemon? Make lemonade the easy way with the KitchenAid® Citrus Juicer attachment. You'll get the last drop of juice from lemons, limes, oranges and grapefruit with a simple twist of the wrist. The juicer has a strainer, too, so seeds and bitter pulp are eliminated.

Once the juicer is attached, place a glass or pitcher under the spout to catch the juice. For small quantities, it may help to prop the glass up closer to the spout on an inverted bowl. Hold the fruit firmly and bring it in contact with the spinning reamer on the juicer. You'll have fresh, pure strained juice in a matter of seconds. Plastic parts of the juicer (everything except the aluminum shaft) are top-rack dishwasher safe to save clean-up time.

Turn Grain into Flour and Taste the Difference Freshness Makes

Grinding wheat, rice, corn, hulled oats or barley is as easy as attaching the Grain Mill to your KitchenAid stand mixer. Fresh flour has a nutty almost sweet flavor that's unmatched by commercially ground product. Wheat flour you mill yourself contains the entire nutritious kernel, including the bran and germ. Consult the instruction book for information on individual grains.

GRAIN MILL NO-NOS

Do not grind grains or nuts that are oily, or those that have a high moisture content, in your Grain Mill. For example, attempting to grind coffee beans, peanuts, sunflower seeds, soybeans or the like could damage the grinding mechanism.

How Many Wheat Berries in One Cup of Flour?

To make wheat flour you will be milling wheat berries, which are whole unprocessed kernels of wheat. One cup of wheat berries yields about 1½ cups of flour. Yields can vary depending on the variety of wheat and when it was harvested among other things. It's best to grind a bit more wheat than you think you will need and store the rest of the flour in an airtight container. Keep it in the refrigerator or freezer, since it is quite perishable.

Wheat berries can be purchased in natural food stores, usually in the bulk section, or ordered online. Hard red winter wheat is the most common variety and is perfect for breads and the other recipes in this book. Soft spring wheat is best used for cakes and cookies. The all-purpose flour sold in sacks in the supermarket is usually a mix of the two types.

CHAPTER 1
BREAKFAST

Basic Cream Scones with Lemon Curd

Makes 8 scones

Lemon Curd (page 19)

2¼ cups all-purpose flour

¼ cup granulated sugar

1 tablespoon baking powder

½ teaspoon salt

6 tablespoons cold butter, cut into pieces

⅔ cup heavy cream

2 eggs

Coarse white decorating sugar

1 Prepare Lemon Curd.

2 Preheat oven to 425°F. Attach flat beater to stand mixer. Combine flour, granulated sugar, baking powder and salt in mixer bowl; mix on low speed 10 seconds. Add butter; mix on low speed 2 minutes or until mixture resembles coarse crumbs.

3 Whisk cream and eggs in small bowl; reserve 1 tablespoon egg mixture. Add remaining egg mixture to flour mixture; mix on low speed just until moistened.

4 Turn out dough onto lightly floured surface. Shape into ball; pat into 8-inch disc. Cut into eight wedges; place 2 inches apart on ungreased baking sheet. Brush reserved egg mixture over tops; sprinkle with coarse sugar.

5 Bake 12 to 14 minutes or until golden. Remove to wire rack to cool. Serve warm.

CHOCOLATE LAVENDER SCONES: Add 1 teaspoon dried lavender to dry ingredients. Stir ½ cup coarsely chopped semisweet chocolate into dough before shaping.

GINGER PEACH SCONES: Stir ⅓ cup chopped dried peaches and 1 tablespoon finely chopped crystallized ginger into dough before shaping.

LEMON POPPY SEED SCONES: Stir grated peel of 1 lemon and 1 tablespoon poppy seeds into dough before shaping. Omit sugar topping. Combine 1 cup powdered sugar and 2 tablespoons lemon juice in small bowl. Drizzle over scones.

MAPLE PECAN SCONES: Stir ½ cup chopped pecans into dough before shaping. Omit sugar topping. Combine ¾ cup powdered sugar and 2 tablespoons maple syrup in small bowl. Drizzle over scones.

Lemon Curd

2 lemons

½ cup sugar

6 tablespoons butter

Pinch of salt

2 eggs, beaten

1 Finely grate lemon peel to measure ½ tablespoon. Attach Citrus Juicer to stand mixer. Juice lemons into liquid measuring cup; measure ⅓ cup juice.

2 Combine sugar, butter, salt, lemon juice and lemon peel in medium saucepan over medium heat, stirring until butter is melted and sugar is dissolved. Gradually whisk in eggs in thin steady stream. Cook over medium-low heat 5 minutes or until thickened to the consistency of pudding, whisking constantly.

3 Strain through fine-mesh sieve into medium bowl. Press plastic wrap onto surface; refrigerate until cold. Transfer to jar with tight-fitting lid or food storage container.

Baked Doughnuts with Cinnamon Glaze

Makes 2 dozen doughnuts and holes

2 cups milk, divided

½ cup (1 stick) butter

5 to 5½ cups all-purpose flour, divided

⅔ cup granulated sugar

2 packages (¼ ounce each) active dry yeast (4½ teaspoons)

1 teaspoon salt

1 teaspoon grated lemon peel

½ teaspoon ground nutmeg

2 eggs

2 cups sifted powdered sugar

½ teaspoon ground cinnamon

1 Combine 1¾ cups milk and butter in small saucepan. Heat over low heat until mixture is 120° to 130°F. (Butter does not need to completely melt.)

2 Attach flat beater to stand mixer. Combine 2 cups flour, granulated sugar, yeast, salt, lemon peel and nutmeg in mixer bowl; mix on low speed 10 seconds. Gradually beat milk mixture into flour mixture on low speed. Increase speed to medium; beat 2 minutes.

3 Beat in eggs and 1 cup flour on low speed. Increase speed to medium; beat 2 minutes. Stir in enough additional flour, about 2 cups, to make soft dough. Cover bowl with greased plastic wrap; refrigerate at least 2 hours or up to 24 hours.

4 Turn out dough onto lightly floured surface. Knead about 1 minute or until no longer sticky, adding remaining ½ cup flour if necessary.

5 Grease two large baking sheets. Roll out dough to ½-inch thickness with lightly floured rolling pin. Cut dough with floured 2½-inch doughnut cutter. Reroll scraps, reserving doughnut holes. Place doughnuts and holes 2 inches apart on prepared baking sheets. Cover and let rise in warm place about 30 minutes or until doubled.

6 Preheat oven to 400°F. Place waxed paper under wire racks. Bake doughnuts and holes 8 to 10 minutes or until golden brown. Remove to prepared wire racks; cool 5 minutes.

7 Combine powdered sugar and cinnamon in small bowl. Stir in enough remaining milk to make pourable glaze. Dip warm doughnuts into glaze. Place on racks, allowing glaze to drip down sides. Serve warm.

Ham and Cheese Grits Soufflé

Makes 4 to 6 servings

2 ounces mozzarella cheese

3 cups water

¾ cup quick-cooking grits

½ teaspoon salt

2 ounces ham, finely chopped

2 tablespoons minced fresh chives

2 eggs, separated

Dash hot pepper sauce

1 Preheat oven to 375°F. Grease 1½-quart soufflé dish or deep round casserole. Assemble Rotor Slicer/Shredder with coarse shredding cone; attach to stand mixer. Shred cheese into medium bowl.

2 Bring water to a boil in medium saucepan over high heat; stir in grits and salt. Reduce heat to medium; cook 5 minutes or until thickened, stirring frequently. Stir in cheese, ham, chives, egg yolks and hot pepper sauce.

3 Remove Rotor Slicer/Shredder; attach wire whip. Whip egg whites in mixer bowl on high speed until stiff peaks form; fold into grits mixture. Spoon into prepared dish.

4 Bake 30 minutes or until puffed and golden. Serve immediately.

Fabulous Feta Frittata

Makes 4 servings

8 eggs

¼ cup chopped fresh basil

¼ cup heavy cream, half-and-half or plain Greek yogurt

¼ teaspoon salt

¼ teaspoon freshly ground black pepper

2 tablespoons butter or olive oil

1 package (4 ounces) crumbled feta cheese with basil, olives and sun-dried tomatoes *or* 1 cup crumbled plain feta cheese

¼ cup pine nuts

1 Preheat broiler.

2 Attach flat beater to stand mixer. Beat eggs, basil, cream, salt and pepper in mixer bowl on medium speed until well blended.

3 Melt butter in large ovenproof skillet over medium heat, tilting skillet to coat bottom and side. Pour egg mixture into skillet. Cover and cook 8 to 10 minutes or until eggs are set around edge (center will be wet).

4 Sprinkle cheese and pine nuts evenly over top. Transfer to broiler; broil 4 to 5 inches from heat source 2 minutes or until center is set and pine nuts are golden brown. Cut into wedges to serve.

NOTE: If skillet is not ovenproof, wrap the handle in heavy-duty foil.

Cherry Buttermilk Loops

Makes 16 rolls

1/3 cup chopped dried
cherries

1/2 cup water

1/2 cup warm buttermilk
(110° to 115°F)

1 egg

3 tablespoons butter,
softened

3 cups bread flour, divided

1/4 cup granulated sugar

2 teaspoons active dry
yeast

1 teaspoon salt

1/4 cup cherry preserves,
large cherry pieces
chopped

1 1/3 cups powdered sugar

3 tablespoons cold
buttermilk

1/4 cup sliced almonds,
toasted*

**To toast almonds, spread in single layer
on baking sheet. Bake in preheated
350°F oven 8 to 10 minutes or until
golden brown, stirring frequently.*

1 Place cherries and water in small microwavable bowl; cover. Microwave on HIGH 30 seconds; let stand 5 minutes. Drain cherries; reserve 1/4 cup soaking liquid in medium bowl. Whisk warm buttermilk, egg and butter into liquid.

2 Attach flat beater to stand mixer. Combine 2 cups flour, granulated sugar, yeast and salt in mixer bowl; mix on low speed 10 seconds. Add buttermilk mixture; mix on medium-low speed until rough dough forms. Replace flat beater with dough hook; knead on low speed 5 to 7 minutes, adding additional 1 cup flour as needed until dough is smooth and elastic. Shape dough into a ball. Place in large lightly greased bowl; turn once to grease surface. Cover and let rise in warm place about 1 hour or until doubled.

3 Lightly grease two baking sheets. Turn out dough onto lightly floured surface. Divide dough into 16 equal pieces. Gently roll and stretch each piece into 7-inch-long rope. Shape each rope into loop with ends crossed; place on prepared baking sheets. Cover and let rise in warm place about 45 minutes or until doubled.

4 Preheat oven to 375°F. Bake 12 to 15 minutes or until golden brown. Meanwhile, heat preserves in small saucepan over low heat until slightly warmed and softened, but not melted. Remove rolls from oven. Immediately brush entire surfaces generously with warm preserves. Remove from baking sheets; cool on wire racks.

5 Combine powdered sugar and cold buttermilk in small bowl, stirring until smooth. Place waxed paper under wire racks. Drizzle icing over rolls. Sprinkle with almonds.

VARIATION: Substitute dried blueberries for dried cherries and blueberry preserves for cherry preserves.

Strawberry Vanilla Jam

Makes 3 half-pint jars

3 pounds fresh strawberries, hulled

1½ cups sugar

4 teaspoons powdered pectin

1 vanilla bean, split and seeds removed

¾ teaspoon lemon juice

3 half-pint canning jars with lids

1 Assemble Juicer and Sauce attachment with high pulp screen; attach to stand mixer. Juice strawberries; reserve juice for another use. Measure 3 cups pulp; place in 5-quart saucepan.

2 Whisk sugar, pectin and vanilla seeds in medium bowl; add to saucepan. Bring to a boil over high heat. Boil 10 minutes, stirring frequently. Stir in lemon juice; cook 5 minutes or until thickened. Jam is done cooking when it forms thick layer on side of pan. Transfer jam to clean, hot jars. Wipe off any jam from top of jars; seal jars with lids and rims.

3 Meanwhile, fill stockpot with enough water to cover jars; bring to a boil over high heat. Reduce heat slightly to stop boiling; carefully lower jars into water. Add additional water to fully submerge jars, if necessary. Return water to a boil; boil 10 minutes. Carefully remove jars from stockpot; cool on kitchen towel. Store sealed jars at room temperature up to 1 year.

Herbed Chicken and Apple Sausages

Makes about 3 pounds

3 pounds boneless chicken thighs with skin, excess fat trimmed, cut into 2-inch strips

1¼ cups (about 3 ounces) chopped dried apples

⅓ cup finely chopped shallots

3 tablespoons frozen apple juice concentrate, thawed

1 tablespoon kosher salt *or* 2¾ teaspoons regular salt

¾ teaspoon freshly ground white or black pepper

1 teaspoon dried sage

1 teaspoon crumbled dried rosemary

½ teaspoon dried thyme

Sausage casings, soaked and drained*

See page 13 of the introduction for more information.

1 Spread chicken on baking sheet. Refrigerate or freeze until slightly firm.

2 Assemble Food Grinder with coarse grinding plate; attach to stand mixer. Grind chicken into mixer bowl. Add dried apples, shallots, apple juice concentrate, salt, pepper, sage, rosemary and thyme; mix well. Cover with plastic wrap and refrigerate 2 hours or until well chilled. Remove and wash grinder.

3 Reassemble grinder with Sausage Stuffer; attach to mixer. Stuff casings with chicken mixture. Refrigerate sausages, uncovered, for at least 4 hours and up to 1 day to cure.

4 Grill, broil or pan-fry sausages until cooked through (165°F). Serve hot.

TIP

This breakfast sausage is equally delicious made into patties. After step 2, form mixture into 3-inch patties. Pan-fry until cooked through (165°F).

French Toast Strata

Makes 6 servings

4 cups (4 ounces) day-old French or Italian bread, cut into large cubes

⅓ cup golden raisins

3 ounces cream cheese, cut into ¼-inch cubes

3 eggs

1½ cups milk

½ cup maple syrup, plus additional for serving

1 teaspoon vanilla

2 tablespoons sugar

1 teaspoon ground cinnamon

1 Grease 11×7-inch baking dish. Place bread cubes in even layer in dish; sprinkle raisins and cream cheese evenly over bread.

2 Attach flat beater to stand mixer. Beat eggs in mixer bowl on medium speed until blended. Add milk, ½ cup maple syrup and vanilla; mix well. Pour egg mixture evenly over bread mixture. Cover; refrigerate at least 4 hours or overnight.

3 Preheat oven to 350°F. Combine sugar and cinnamon in small bowl; sprinkle evenly over strata.

4 Bake, uncovered, 40 to 45 minutes or until puffed, golden brown and knife inserted into center comes out clean. Cut into squares. Serve warm with additional maple syrup.

Apple and Raisin Oven Pancake

Makes 6 servings

1 large baking apple, peeled, cored and quartered

⅓ cup raisins

2 tablespoons packed brown sugar

½ teaspoon ground cinnamon

4 eggs

⅔ cup milk

⅔ cup all-purpose flour

2 tablespoons butter, melted

Powdered sugar (optional)

1 Preheat oven to 350°F. Grease 9-inch pie plate.

2 Assemble Food Processor attachment with adjustable slicing disc. Slide lever to sixth notch for thick slices; attach to stand mixer. Slice apple quarters lengthwise into medium bowl. Stir in raisins, brown sugar and cinnamon; transfer to prepared pie plate.

3 Bake 10 to 15 minutes or until apple begins to soften. Remove from oven. *Increase oven temperature to 450°F.*

4 Meanwhile, remove Food Processor; attach wire whip. Whip eggs, milk, flour and butter in mixer bowl on medium-low speed until blended. Pour batter over apple mixture.

5 Bake 15 minutes or until pancake is golden brown. Sprinkle with powdered sugar, if desired.

Italian Sausage and Arugula Frittata

Makes 4 servings

⅛ red onion

1 roasted red pepper

12 cremini mushrooms

1 ounce Asiago cheese

1 tablespoon olive oil

2 links sweet Italian turkey sausage

1 cup chopped arugula

8 eggs

½ teaspoon salt

¼ teaspoon freshly ground black pepper

1 Preheat oven to 350°F. Grease four 6-ounce ramekins or custard cups; place on baking sheet.

2 Assemble Food Processor attachment with dicing disc; attach to stand mixer. Dice onion into small bowl. Dice red pepper into separate small bowl. Replace dicing disc with slicing disc; slide lever to third notch for medium slices. Slice mushrooms into medium bowl. Replace slicing disc with shredding disc; shred cheese into another small bowl.

3 Heat oil in medium skillet over medium heat. Remove sausage from casings; add to skillet. Cook until lightly browned, stirring to break up sausage. Add onion; sauté 1 minute or until softened. Add mushrooms; sauté 5 minutes. Stir in arugula and roasted peppers; sauté 1 minute or until heated through. Divide mixture evenly among prepared ramekins.

4 Remove Food Processor; attach wire whip. Whip eggs, salt and black pepper in mixer bowl on medium speed until well blended. Pour over sausage mixture; sprinkle with cheese.

5 Bake 25 to 30 minutes or until centers are set. Cool 10 minutes; frittata will deflate slightly. Serve warm or at room temperature.

Orange Cinnamon Rolls

Makes 18 rolls

1 package (¼ ounce) active dry yeast (2¼ teaspoons)

¼ cup warm water (120°F)

½ cup warm milk (120°F)

¼ cup granulated sugar

5 tablespoons butter, melted, divided

1 egg

1 teaspoon grated orange peel

1 teaspoon vanilla

½ teaspoon salt

2½ to 2¾ cups all-purpose flour, divided

½ cup packed brown sugar

1 tablespoon ground cinnamon

⅓ cup raisins (optional)

½ cup powdered sugar

1 to 2 tablespoons fresh orange juice

1 Attach flat beater to stand mixer. Combine yeast and warm water in mixer bowl; stir to dissolve. Let stand 5 minutes or until bubbly.

2 Add milk, granulated sugar, 2 tablespoons butter, egg, orange peel, vanilla and salt; beat on medium speed until blended. Add 2½ cups flour; beat until soft dough forms.

3 Replace flat beater with dough hook; knead on low speed 5 to 7 minutes or until dough is smooth and elastic, adding enough remaining flour 1 tablespoon at a time to prevent sticking.

4 Shape dough into a ball. Place dough in large lightly greased bowl; turn once to grease surface. Cover and let rise in warm place about 1 hour or until doubled.

5 Grease two 8-inch round cake pans. Combine brown sugar, 1 tablespoon butter and cinnamon in small bowl.

6 Punch down dough. Roll out dough into 18×8-inch rectangle on lightly floured surface. Brush with remaining 2 tablespoons butter; spread brown sugar mixture evenly over dough, leaving 1-inch border. Sprinkle with raisins, if desired. Starting with long side, roll up dough tightly; pinch seam to seal. Cut crosswise into 1-inch slices; arrange slices cut sides up in prepared pans. Cover loosely and let rise in warm place 30 to 40 minutes or until almost doubled. Preheat oven to 350°F.

7 Bake 18 minutes or until golden brown. Remove to wire racks to cool slightly.

8 Whisk powdered sugar and 1 tablespoon orange juice in small bowl until smooth. Add additional juice if necessary to reach desired consistency. Drizzle glaze over warm rolls.

Egg Bagels

Makes 1 dozen bagels

½ cup warm water (120°F), divided

1 package (¼ ounce) active dry yeast (2¼ teaspoons)

2 tablespoons plus 1 teaspoon sugar, divided

2½ to 3 cups all-purpose flour, divided

2 eggs, divided

1 tablespoon canola oil

1 teaspoon salt

2 tablespoons cold water

Cream cheese (optional)

1 Attach flat beater to stand mixer. Combine ¼ cup warm water, yeast and 1 teaspoon sugar in mixer bowl; stir to dissolve yeast. Let stand 5 minutes or until bubbly.

2 Add 2 cups flour, 1 egg, oil, salt and ¼ cup warm water; mix on low speed 1 minute or until soft dough forms. Replace flat beater with dough hook; knead on low speed 5 to 7 minutes, or until dough is smooth and elastic, adding additional flour 1 tablespoon at a time to prevent sticking, if necessary.

3 Shape dough into a ball. Place dough in large lightly greased bowl; turn once to grease surface. Cover and let stand in warm place 15 minutes.

4 Grease baking sheet. Turn out dough onto lightly floured surface. Shape dough into 6-inch-long pieces; form into rings and pinch ends to seal. Place on prepared baking sheet; let stand 15 minutes.

5 Preheat oven to 425°F. Combine 8 cups water and remaining 2 tablespoons sugar in large saucepan or Dutch oven; bring to a boil over medium-high heat. Working in batches, gently place bagels in boiling water; cook 1 minute, turning once. Remove bagels from water using slotted spoon to same baking sheet.

6 Beat remaining egg and 2 tablespoons cold water in small bowl. Brush evenly over bagels.

7 Bake 20 to 25 minutes or until golden brown. Remove to wire racks; cool completely. Serve with cream cheese, if desired.

CHAPTER 2
JUICE AND COFFEE

Sweet and Sour Juice

Makes 2 servings

⅛ papaya

½ grapefruit, peeled

1½ cups fresh raspberries

1 Assemble Juicer and Sauce attachment with high pulp screen; attach to stand mixer. Cut papaya and grapefruit to fit in feed tube.

2 Juice raspberries, papaya and grapefruit. Stir; serve immediately.

Spicy-Sweet Grapefruit Juice

Makes 3 servings

2 grapefruits, peeled

5 carrots

1 inch fresh ginger, peeled

1 Assemble Juicer and Sauce attachment with low pulp screen; attach to stand mixer. Cut grapefruits to fit in feed tube.

2 Juice grapefruits, carrots and ginger. Stir; serve immediately.

Viennese Coffee

Makes about 4 servings

1 cup heavy cream, divided

1 teaspoon powdered sugar

3 ounces bittersweet or semisweet chocolate, chopped

3 cups strong freshly brewed hot coffee

¼ cup crème de cacao or Irish cream (optional)

Chocolate shavings (optional)

1 Chill stand mixer bowl and wire whip. Attach wire whip to stand mixer. Place ⅔ cup cream and sugar in chilled bowl. Whip on high speed until soft peaks form.

2 Place remaining ⅓ cup cream in small heavy saucepan. Bring to a simmer over medium-low heat. Add chopped chocolate; cover and remove from heat. Let stand 5 minutes or until chocolate is melted; stir until smooth.

3 Add hot coffee to chocolate mixture. Heat over low heat just until bubbles form around edge of pan, stirring frequently. Remove from heat; stir in crème de cacao, if desired. Pour into mugs. Top with whipped cream and garnish with chocolate shavings.

Citus Sprout Juice

Makes 2 servings

- 1 orange, peeled
- 1 cup brussels sprouts
- 4 leaves romaine lettuce
- ½ apple
- ½ lemon, peeled

1 Assemble Juicer and Sauce attachment with low pulp screen; attach to stand mixer. Cut orange to fit in feed tube.

2 Juice brussels sprouts, romaine, orange, apple and lemon. Stir; serve immediately.

Apple, Sweet Potato and Carrot Juice

Makes 4 servings

- 4 apples
- 1 sweet potato
- 1 carrot

1 Assemble Juicer and Sauce attachment with low pulp screen; attach to stand mixer. Cut apples and sweet potato to fit in feed tube.

2 Juice apples, sweet potato and carrot. Stir; serve immediately.

Pomegranate-Orange Juice

Makes 8 servings

- 4 oranges, halved
- 3 cups pomegranate juice
- 1 cup cranberry juice
- 2 cups cold club soda

1 Attach Citrus Juicer to stand mixer. Juice oranges into pitcher. Stir in pomegranate juice and cranberry juice.

2 Refrigerate 30 minutes or until cold. Stir in club soda just before serving. Serve in ice-filled glasses.

Pink Power Juice

Makes 2 servings

- ¼ small watermelon, rind removed
- 1 tomato
- 1 lemon, peeled

1 Assemble Juicer and Sauce attachment with low pulp screen; attach to stand mixer. Cut watermelon, tomato and lemon to fit in feed tube.

2 Juice watermelon, tomato and lemon. Stir; serve immediately.

Mexican Coffee with Chocolate and Cinnamon

Makes 6 servings

6 cups water

½ cup ground dark roast coffee

2 cinnamon sticks

1 cup half-and-half

⅓ cup chocolate syrup

¼ cup packed dark brown sugar

1½ teaspoons vanilla, divided

1 cup heavy cream

¼ cup powdered sugar

Ground cinnamon

1 Chill stand mixer bowl and wire whip.

2 Place water in drip coffee maker. Place coffee and cinnamon sticks in coffee filter. Combine half-and-half, chocolate syrup, brown sugar and 1 teaspoon vanilla in coffee pot. Place coffee pot in coffee maker; brew coffee into pot with cream mixture.

3 Meanwhile, attach wire whip to stand mixer. Whip cream in chilled mixer bowl on high speed until soft peaks form. Add powdered sugar and remaining ½ teaspoon vanilla; beat until stiff peaks form.

4 Pour coffee into coffee cups; top with dollop of whipped cream. Sprinkle with ground cinnamon.

Citrus Cooler

Makes 9 servings

6 oranges, halved

2 cups unsweetened pineapple juice

1 teaspoon lemon juice

¾ teaspoon coconut extract

¾ teaspoon vanilla

2 cups cold sparkling water

1 Attach Citrus Juicer to stand mixer. Juice oranges into large pitcher. Stir in pineapple juice, lemon juice, coconut extract and vanilla. Refrigerate 30 minutes or until cold.

2 Stir in sparkling water just before serving. Serve in ice-filled glasses.

Mexican Coffee
with Chocolate
and Cinnamon

CHAPTER 3
APPETIZERS AND SNACKS

Sausage-Stuffed Mushrooms

Makes 30 appetizers

½ pound pork shoulder, trimmed and cut into 2-inch strips

30 cremini mushrooms

1 slice white bread

1 tablespoon chopped fresh parsley, plus additional for garnish

¾ teaspoon salt

¼ teaspoon dried sage

⅛ teaspoon freshly ground black pepper

4 ounces mozzarella cheese, partially frozen

1 Spread pork on baking sheet; refrigerate or freeze until slightly firm. Remove stems from mushrooms; set caps aside. Assemble Food Grinder with coarse grinding plate; attach to stand mixer. Grind mushroom stems into medium bowl. Grind bread into small bowl; set aside.

2 Preheat oven to 450°F. Grind pork into mixer bowl. Add 1 tablespoon parsley, salt, sage and pepper. Remove Food Grinder; attach flat beater. Mix on low speed 1 minute or until well combined.

3 Brown sausage mixture in medium skillet over medium heat; transfer to bowl with slotted spoon. Add mushroom stems to drippings in skillet; sauté 3 minutes. Remove from heat.

4 Assemble Rotor Slicer/Shredder with fine shredding cone; attach to mixer. Shred cheese into bowl; add mushroom stems, bread crumbs and sausage.

5 Fill mushroom caps with sausage mixture. Place on baking sheets. Bake 15 minutes or until heated through. Garnish with additional parsley.

Mango and Red Pepper Salsa

Makes 3 cups salsa

5 mangoes, pitted and peeled

2 red bell peppers, halved and seeded

¼ small red onion

1 jalapeño pepper, halved and seeded

1 clove garlic

¼ cup packed cilantro leaves, finely chopped

1 tablespoon fresh lime juice

1½ teaspoons sugar

1 teaspoon coarse salt

Tortilla chips

1 Assemble Food Processor attachment with dicing disc; attach to stand mixer. Dice mangoes, bell peppers, onion, jalapeño and garlic into mixer bowl.

2 Stir in cilantro, lime juice, sugar and salt. Serve with tortilla chips.

Chipotle Chicken Quesadillas

Makes 5 servings

1¼ pounds boneless skinless chicken breasts

1 teaspoon salt

3 cloves garlic, crushed

4 ounces Monterey Jack cheese, partially frozen

4 ounces Cheddar cheese, partially frozen

1 package (8 ounces) cream cheese, softened

1 tablespoon minced chipotle pepper in adobo sauce

5 (10-inch) flour tortillas

2½ teaspoons vegetable oil

Guacamole, sour cream, salsa and chopped fresh cilantro

1 Place chicken in single layer in large deep skillet. Sprinkle with salt; add cold water to cover by 1 inch. Add garlic to water. Bring to a boil over high heat. Reduce heat to maintain a simmer; cover and cook 10 to 15 minutes until chicken is cooked through (165°F). Transfer chicken to cutting board to cool.

2 Assemble Rotor Slicer/Shredder with fine shredding cone; attach to stand mixer. Shred Monterey Jack cheese and Cheddar cheese into mixer bowl; transfer half of cheese to small bowl. Replace fine shredding cone with coarse shredding cone; shred chicken into separate large bowl. Remove Rotor Slicer/Shredder; attach flat beater.

3 Add cream cheese and chipotle pepper to mixer bowl with shredded cheese; beat on medium speed 1 minute until blended. Spread cheese mixture evenly over half of each tortilla; top evenly with chicken and reserved shredded cheese. Fold tortillas in half.

4 Heat ½ teaspoon oil in large skillet over medium-high heat. Cook one to two quesadillas at a time 2 to 3 minutes per side or until lightly browned, turning once and adding additional oil as needed.

5 Cut each quesadilla into four wedges. Serve with guacamole, sour cream, salsa and cilantro.

Pot Stickers

Makes about 3 dozen pot stickers

- 2 cups all-purpose flour
- ¾ cup plus 2 tablespoons boiling water
- ½ head napa cabbage, cored
- 8 ounces ground pork
- 2 tablespoons finely chopped water chestnuts
- 1 green onion, finely chopped
- 1½ teaspoons cornstarch
- 1½ teaspoons dry sherry
- 1½ teaspoons soy sauce
- ½ teaspoon minced fresh ginger
- ½ teaspoon dark sesame oil
- ¼ teaspoon sugar
- 2 tablespoons vegetable oil
- ⅔ cup chicken broth

   Rice wine vinegar, chili oil and additional soy sauce

1 Attach dough hook to stand mixer. Place flour in mixer bowl; make well in center. Pour in boiling water; stir with wooden spoon until dough forms. Knead on low speed 5 minutes or until dough is smooth and satiny. Shape dough into a ball; wrap with plastic wrap and let rest 30 minutes.

2 Remove dough hook. Assemble Rotor Slicer/Shredder with coarse shredding cone; attach to stand mixer. Shred cabbage into mixer bowl; measure ½ cup. Combine ½ cup cabbage, pork, water chestnuts, onion, cornstarch, sherry, 1½ teaspoons soy sauce, ginger, sesame oil and sugar in mixer bowl; mix well.

3 Divide dough in half; wrap half with plastic wrap. Roll out remaining half of dough to ⅛-inch thickness on lightly floured surface. Cut out 3-inch circles with round cookie cutter. Place 1 rounded teaspoon filling in center of each circle.

4 To shape each pot sticker, lightly moisten edges of dough circles with water; fold in half. Pinch edges to seal, making pleats. Place seam side up on baking sheet, pressing to make flat base; cover. Repeat with remaining dough and filling.*

5 Heat 1 tablespoon vegetable oil in large nonstick skillet over medium heat. Place half of pot stickers in skillet, seam side up. Cook 5 to 6 minutes or until bottoms are golden brown.

6 Pour in ⅓ cup broth. Reduce heat to low; cover tightly and simmer about 10 minutes or until liquid is absorbed. Repeat with remaining vegetable oil, dumplings and broth. Serve warm with vinegar, chili oil and additional soy sauce for dipping.

Pot stickers may be refrigerated at this point up to 4 hours or frozen for longer storage. (Do not thaw frozen pot stickers before cooking.)

Prosciutto-Wrapped Figs with Orange-Honey Sauce

Makes 8 servings

16 dried Mission figs

8 slices prosciutto, at room temperature

1 orange

½ lemon

1 tablespoon honey

Red pepper flakes

Salt (optional)

1 Place figs in small saucepan; cover with water. Bring to a boil over medium-high heat. Reduce heat; cover and simmer 8 minutes or until figs are soft. Drain and set aside to cool.

2 Meanwhile, cut prosciutto slices in half lengthwise. Wrap each fig with prosciutto strip; secure with toothpick. Arrange on serving plate.

3 Attach Citrus Juicer to stand mixer. Juice orange into small bowl; measure 6 tablespoons juice. Juice lemon into another small bowl; measure 2 teaspoons juice.

4 Combine 6 tablespoons orange juice, 2 teaspoons lemon juice, honey, red pepper flakes and salt, if desired, in small saucepan. Bring to a boil over medium-high heat. Cook 2 minutes or until mixture is syrupy and reduced by half. Drizzle some of sauce over figs; serve remaining sauce for dipping.

Okonomiyaki (Savory Pancake)

Makes 4 servings

¼ cup ketchup

2 tablespoons sake

1½ tablespoons Worcestershire sauce

1 teaspoon tamari or soy sauce

¼ teaspoon Dijon mustard

1 small green cabbage, quartered and cored

⅓ cup corn

⅓ cup chopped mushrooms

⅓ cup chopped red bell pepper

2 eggs

1 cup all-purpose flour

½ teaspoon salt

2 green onions, chopped

¾ cup water

4 teaspoons vegetable oil

¼ cup chopped cooked chicken (optional)

Mayonnaise (optional)

1 Preheat oven to 200°F. Place wire rack on baking sheet; place in oven. For sauce, combine ketchup, sake, Worcestershire sauce, tamari and mustard in small saucepan over medium-low heat. Simmer 1 minute, stirring constantly. Remove from heat; cool to room temperature.

2 Assemble Rotor Slicer/Shredder with coarse shredding cone; attach to stand mixer. Shred cabbage into large bowl; measure 1 cup. Combine corn, mushrooms and bell pepper in small bowl.

3 Remove Rotor Slicer/Shredder; attach flat beater. Combine eggs, flour and salt in mixer bowl; mix on medium-low speed until combined but still lumpy. Stir in 1 cup cabbage, green onions and water on low speed. Add additional water if needed to make thick batter.

4 Heat large nonstick skillet or griddle over medium-high heat. Brush skillet with 1 teaspoon oil. Add ¼ cup batter; press into 5-inch circle with bottom of measuring cup. Cook 2 minutes; top with ¼ cup vegetable mixture and 1 tablespoon chicken, if desired, pressing filling into pancake with spatula. Cook 2 to 3 minutes until edges of pancake look dull and bottom is lightly browned. Turn pancake and cook 2 to 4 minutes or until cooked through. Keep warm on wire rack in oven; repeat with remaining batter and filling.

5 Cut pancakes into wedges; drizzle with some of sauce. Serve warm with remaining sauce and mayonnaise, if desired.

TIP

Okonomiyaki is a favorite Japanese snack food, enjoyed like pizza in bars and restaurants. Use any vegetables or protein for the filling; try asparagus, onions, zucchini, ham, tofu or roast beef.

Manchego Cheese Croquettes

Makes 6 servings

2 ounces manchego or Parmesan cheese

¼ cup (½ stick) butter

1 tablespoon minced shallot or onion

½ cup all-purpose flour

¾ cup milk

¼ teaspoon salt

¼ teaspoon smoked paprika or regular paprika

⅛ teaspoon ground nutmeg

1 egg

½ cup panko or plain dry bread crumbs

Vegetable oil for frying

1 Assemble Food Processor attachment with shredding disc; attach to stand mixer. Shred cheese into medium bowl.

2 Melt butter in medium skillet over medium heat. Add shallot; cook and stir 2 minutes. Stir in flour; cook and stir 2 minutes. Gradually whisk in milk; cook until mixture comes to a boil. Remove from heat. Stir in ¼ cup shredded cheese, salt, paprika and nutmeg. Transfer mixture to small bowl; cover and refrigerate several hours or up to 24 hours.

3 Line baking sheet with parchment paper. Shape teaspoonfuls of dough into 1-inch balls with lightly floured hands; place on prepared baking sheet. Beat egg in shallow bowl. Combine bread crumbs and remaining shredded cheese in another shallow bowl. Dip each ball into egg, then roll in bread crumb mixture.

4 Heat ¼ cup oil in medium skillet over medium-high heat. Cook croquettes in batches until brown on all sides, adding additional oil as needed. Drain on paper towels. Serve warm.

NOTE: Cooked croquettes may be kept warm in a 200°F oven up to 30 minutes before serving.

CHAPTER 4
PASTA

Spinach Pasta Pomodoro

1 recipe Spinach Pasta Dough (page 80), cut into fettuccine

5 large tomatoes, cut into sixths

3 tablespoons olive oil

3 cloves garlic, minced

½ cup chopped fresh basil

1 teaspoon sugar

1 teaspoon salt

¼ teaspoon freshly ground black pepper

Shredded Parmesan cheese

Makes 4 servings

1 Prepare Spinach Pasta Dough.

2 Assemble Fruit/Vegetable Strainer; attach to stand mixer. Strain tomatoes into mixer bowl. Measure 3 cups puree.

3 Heat oil in medium saucepan over medium heat. Add garlic; sauté 2 minutes. Add tomato puree, basil, sugar, salt and pepper. Reduce heat; cover and simmer 30 minutes.

4 Bring large pot of salted water to a boil. Cook fettuccine 2 minutes or until tender, stirring frequently. Drain. Serve sauce over pasta; top with Parmesan cheese.

Baked Spinach and Mushroom Fettuccine

Makes 4 servings

8 ounces Spinach Pasta Dough (page 80), cut into fettuccine

8 ounces white or cremini mushrooms

2 ounces Swiss cheese, partially frozen

1 tablespoon vegetable oil

2 green onions, finely chopped

1 teaspoon minced garlic

10 ounces fresh baby spinach, coarsely chopped

2 tablespoons water

1 container (15 ounces) ricotta cheese

¾ cup heavy cream

1 egg

½ teaspoon salt

½ teaspoon ground mace or nutmeg

½ teaspoon freshly ground black pepper

1 Prepare pasta. Assemble Food Processor with adjustable slicing disc; attach to stand mixer. Slice mushrooms vertically into thick slices into medium bowl. Replace adjustable slicing disc with shredding disc; shred Swiss cheese into small bowl.

2 Preheat oven to 350°F. Spray 1½-quart casserole with nonstick cooking spray. Bring large saucepan of salted water to a boil. Add pasta; cook 2 minutes or until barely tender. Drain well.

3 Heat oil in medium skillet over medium heat. Add mushrooms, green onions and garlic; sauté until mushrooms are softened. Add spinach and 2 tablespoons water. Cover and cook about 3 minutes or until spinach is wilted.

4 Combine ricotta cheese, cream, egg, salt, mace and pepper in large bowl. Gently stir in noodles and vegetables until coated evenly. Spread mixture in prepared casserole. Sprinkle with Swiss cheese.

5 Bake 25 to 30 minutes or until knife inserted halfway into center comes out clean.

Pasta with Caramelized Onions and Goat Cheese

Makes 4 to 6 servings

6 sweet onions, halved

1 tablespoon olive oil

12 ounces uncooked campanelle, orecchiette or farfalle pasta

2 cloves garlic, minced

¼ cup white wine or vegetable broth

3 teaspoons chopped fresh sage *or* 1 teaspoon dried sage

1 teaspoon salt

¼ teaspoon freshly ground black pepper

1 package (4 ounces) crumbled goat cheese

½ cup milk

½ cup walnut halves, toasted*

*To toast walnuts, spread in single layer in heavy skillet. Cook over medium heat 1 to 2 minutes or until nuts are lightly browned, stirring frequently.

1 Assemble Rotor Slicer/Shredder with thick slicing cone; attach to stand mixer. Slice onions into mixer bowl.

2 Heat oil in Dutch oven or large skillet over medium heat. Add onions; cook 20 to 25 minutes or until golden and caramelized, stirring occasionally and adding water by tablespoons if onions are too dry.

3 Meanwhile, cook pasta according to package directions. Drain; keep warm.

4 Add garlic to onions in Dutch oven; cook 3 minutes or until softened. Add wine, sage, salt and pepper; cook until liquid has evaporated. Remove from heat. Add pasta, goat cheese and milk; stir until cheese is melted. Sprinkle with walnuts.

Pasta Bolognese

 + +

2 tablespoons olive oil

1½ pounds ground beef

½ pound ground pork

2 carrots, cut into 1-inch pieces

2 stalks celery, cut into 1-inch pieces

1 large onion, cut into wedges

¼ cup fresh parsley sprigs

3 cloves garlic

6 large ripe tomatoes, cut into sixths

¼ cup water

¼ cup red wine

2 tablespoons tomato paste

1½ teaspoons salt

1 teaspoon dried basil

1 teaspoon dried oregano

1 bay leaf

¼ teaspoon freshly ground black pepper

1 recipe Egg Pasta Dough (page 79), cut into linguine

Shredded Parmesan cheese

Makes 4 to 6 servings

1 Heat oil in large skillet over medium heat. Add beef, pork, carrots, celery, onion, parsley and garlic. Sauté 20 minutes. Remove from heat; cool 10 minutes.

2 Assemble Food Grinder with coarse grinding plate; attach to stand mixer. Grind meat mixture into Dutch oven or large saucepan. Remove Food Grinder. Assemble Fruit/Vegetable Strainer; attach to mixer. Strain tomatoes into large measuring cup; measure 4 cups puree.

3 Add tomato puree, water, wine, tomato paste, salt, basil, oregano, bay leaf and pepper to meat mixture. Cover and simmer over medium-low heat 1 hour.

4 Meanwhile, prepare pasta. Bring large pot of salted water to a boil. Add pasta and cook 2 minutes or until barely tender, stirring frequently. Drain. Serve sauce over pasta; top with Parmesan cheese.

Shells and Fontina

8 ounces uncooked pasta shells *or* ½ recipe Eggless Dough for Pasta Press (page 81), cut into large macaroni

5½ ounces fontina cheese, partially frozen

3 ounces Parmesan cheese

1¾ cups milk

4 large fresh sage leaves

3 tablespoons butter

¼ cup all-purpose flour

½ cup tomato sauce

Salt and freshly ground black pepper

¼ cup plain dry bread crumbs

1 Prepare pasta with Pasta Press, if desired. Assemble Food Processor with shredding disc; attach to stand mixer. Shred fontina cheese into medium bowl. Shred Parmesan cheese into small bowl.

2 Preheat oven to 350°F. Bring large pot of salted water to a boil. Cook fresh macaroni 2 to 3 minutes or dried shells according to package directions until al dente. Run under cold running water to stop cooking; drain.

3 Meanwhile, heat milk with sage leaves in small saucepan over medium heat; do not boil. Melt butter in large saucepan over medium-low heat until bubbly. Whisk in flour until smooth; cook 2 minutes without browning, whisking frequently. Remove sage and gradually whisk in milk. Increase heat to medium; cook 4 to 5 minutes, whisking constantly until mixture begins to bubble and thickens slightly. Stir in tomato sauce and season with salt and pepper. Remove from heat; stir in ½ cup Parmesan cheese until smooth.

4 Add pasta to sauce; stir to coat. Spoon one third of pasta mixture into 2-quart casserole. Top with one third of shredded fontina. Repeat layers twice. Sprinkle with bread crumbs and remaining Parmesan cheese.

5 Bake 20 to 25 minutes or until hot and bubbly.

Beef and Sausage Lasagna

Makes 10 servings

2 tablespoons olive oil

1 large yellow onion, chopped

2 cloves garlic, minced

1 pound ground beef

1 pound sweet Italian sausage, casings removed

1 can (28 ounces) crushed tomatoes

1 can (8 ounce) tomato sauce

1 can (6 ounces) tomato paste

1 cup hearty red wine

½ cup water

1 teaspoon dried basil

1 teaspoon dried oregano

1¼ teaspoons salt, divided

¼ teaspoon red pepper flakes

1 dried bay leaf

1 recipe Egg Pasta Dough or Semolina Pasta Dough (page 79)

16 ounces mozzarella cheese, partially frozen

4 ounces Parmesan cheese

1 container (32 ounces) ricotta cheese

2 eggs, beaten

¼ teaspoon freshly ground black pepper

1 For sauce, heat 2 tablespoons oil in Dutch oven or large saucepan over medium-high heat. Add onion; sauté about 3 minutes or until softened. Add garlic; cook 1 minute or until fragrant. Add beef and sausage; cook about 10 minutes or until no longer pink, stirring to break up meat. Add tomatoes, tomato sauce, tomato paste, wine, water, basil, oregano, ¾ teaspoon salt, red pepper flakes and bay leaf; bring to simmer, scraping up browned bits with spoon. Reduce heat to medium-low; simmer, uncovered, 1 hour or until reduced by one fourth, stirring frequently. Discard bay leaf.

2 Meanwhile, prepare pasta dough. Cut pasta into 5×4-inch noodles with sharp knife. Arrange in single layer on kitchen towel; let rest 10 minutes.

3 Meanwhile, preheat oven to 350°F. Grease 15×10-inch baking dish. Bring large pot of salted water to boil. Add lasagna noodles and cook 2 minutes or until barely tender, stirring frequently. Drain and transfer pasta to bowl of cold water to cool. Drain again and arrange in single layer on clean kitchen towels to remove excess water.

4 Assemble Rotor Slicer/Shredder with coarse shredding cone; attach to mixer. Shred mozzarella cheese into large bowl. Replace coarse shredding cone with fine shredding cone; shred Parmesan cheese into medium bowl.

5 For filling, mix ricotta cheese, ½ cup Parmesan cheese, eggs, remaining ½ teaspoon salt and pepper in large bowl. Spread 1 cup sauce in baking dish. Layer with four lasagna noodles,

slightly overlapping. Spread with one third of sauce, half of filling and 2 cups of mozzarella cheese. Repeat with four more noodles, half of remaining sauce, remaining filling and 2 cups mozzarella. Finish with four noodles and sauce and sprinkle with remaining Parmesan cheese.

Cover with greased foil. (Lasagna can be cooled, covered and refrigerated for 1 day.)

6 Place dish on baking sheet. Bake 30 minutes. Uncover; bake 20 to 30 minutes more (30 to 40 minutes for chilled lasagna) or until sauce is bubbly. Let stand 15 minutes before serving.

Italian Three-Cheese Macaroni

Makes 4 servings

½ recipe Eggless Dough for Pasta Press (page 81), cut into small macaroni *or* 2 cups uncooked elbow macaroni

3 ounces Cheddar cheese, partially frozen

1 ounce Parmesan cheese

4 ounces mozzarella cheese, partially frozen

3 tablespoons butter

3 tablespoons all-purpose flour

1 teaspoon dried Italian seasoning

½ teaspoon salt

¼ teaspoon freshly ground black pepper

1¾ cups milk

1 can (about 14 ounces) diced tomatoes, drained

½ cup plain dry bread crumbs

1 Prepare pasta with Pasta Press. Assemble Food Processor attachment with shredding disc; attach to stand mixer. Shred Cheddar and Parmesan cheeses into mixer bowl. Shred mozzarella cheese into medium bowl.

2 Preheat oven to 350°F. Spray 2-quart round casserole with nonstick cooking spray.

3 Bring large pot of salted water to a boil. Cook fresh macaroni 2 to 3 minutes or dried macaroni according to package directions until al dente. Drain and set aside.

4 Melt butter in medium saucepan over medium heat. Whisk in flour, Italian seasoning, salt and pepper until smooth. Gradually add milk, whisking constantly until slightly thickened. Add Cheddar cheese and Parmesan cheese; stir until smooth.

5 Layer half of pasta, half of tomatoes and half of cheese sauce in prepared dish. Repeat layers. Sprinkle with mozzarella cheese and bread crumbs.

6 Cover and bake 30 minutes or until heated through. Uncover and bake 5 minutes or until top is golden brown.

Spinach and Mushroom Cannelloni

Makes 6 to 8 servings

1 recipe Egg Pasta Dough (page 79)

18 ounces fresh spinach*

2 tablespoons olive oil

8 ounces cremini mushrooms, chopped

1 small onion, finely chopped

1 clove garlic, minced

1 cup ricotta cheese

1 cup shredded Parmesan cheese, divided

1 egg, beaten

½ teaspoon salt

½ teaspoon freshly ground black pepper

¼ teaspoon ground nutmeg, divided

3 cups whole milk

1 dried bay leaf

8 tablespoons butter, divided, plus additional for baking dish

⅓ cup all-purpose flour

Shredded fresh basil

Two 10-ounce packages chopped frozen spinach, thawed and squeezed dry, can be substituted for the fresh spinach. Proceed to step 2.

1 Prepare pasta dough. For filling, rinse spinach and shake dry; place in large saucepan with water clinging to leaves. Cover and cook over medium heat 7 minutes or until wilted and tender, stirring occasionally. Drain; rinse under cold running water until cool. Squeeze all excess liquid from spinach a handful at a time. Chop spinach and place in large bowl.

2 Heat olive oil in large skillet over medium-high heat. Add mushrooms; cook 6 minutes or until they give off their liquid, stirring occasionally. Add onion and garlic; cook about 5 minutes until mushroom liquid is evaporated, stirring occasionally. Transfer to bowl with spinach; let cool. Stir in ricotta cheese, ½ cup Parmesan cheese, egg, salt, pepper and ⅛ teaspoon nutmeg.

3 For sauce, bring milk and bay leaf to a simmer in medium saucepan over medium heat. Melt 5 tablespoons butter in heavy medium saucepan over medium heat. Whisk in flour; reduce heat to medium-low. Let bubble without browning 1 minute. Whisk in hot milk with bay leaf. Bring to simmer, whisking often; simmer 5 minutes or until slightly reduced. Remove and discard bay leaf. Add remaining ⅛ teaspoon nutmeg and season with salt and pepper. Dot top of sauce with 1 tablespoon butter to prevent skin from forming.

4 Roll pasta dough to thickness setting 5. Cut into 5-inch squares with sharp knife; place in single layer on floured surface. Let rest 10 minutes.

5 Preheat oven to 350°F. Bring large pot of salted water to a boil. Add pasta squares and cook 2 minutes or until barely tender, stirring frequently to prevent sticking.

Drain and transfer pasta to bowl of cold water to cool. Place pasta squares on clean kitchen towels to remove excess water.

6 Grease large baking dish with 1 tablespoon butter. Spread about ½ cup cream sauce in prepared baking dish. Place 1 pasta square on work surface; spoon 3 tablespoons filling along bottom edge and roll up. Place seam side down in baking dish. Repeat with remaining filling and pasta. Spread remaining sauce over pasta. Sprinkle with remaining ½ cup Parmesan and dot with remaining 1 tablespoon butter. (Cannelloni can be cooled, covered and refrigerated for up to 8 hours.)

7 Bake about 25 minutes (35 minutes for chilled cannelloni) or until sauce is bubbling and top is golden brown. Let stand 5 minutes before serving. Garnish with shredded basil.

Pesto Pasta with Asparagus and Tomatoes

Makes 4 servings

1 cup packed fresh basil leaves

½ cup pine nuts, toasted*

½ cup shredded Parmesan cheese, divided

2 cloves garlic

½ teaspoon salt

¼ teaspoon freshly ground black pepper

¼ cup olive oil

1 medium tomato, chopped

8 ounces asparagus spears, cut into 2-inch pieces

½ recipe Eggless Dough for Pasta Press (page 81), cut into spaghetti

Place pine nuts in small saucepan. Heat over low heat 2 minutes or until light brown and fragrant, shaking occasionally.

1 Place basil, pine nuts, ¼ cup cheese, garlic, salt and pepper in food processor; drizzle with 1 tablespoon olive oil. Process about 10 seconds or until coarsely chopped. With motor running, drizzle in remaining 3 tablespoons olive oil. Process about 30 seconds or until almost smooth. Transfer to medium bowl; stir in tomato.

2 Prepare pasta with Pasta Press. Bring large pot of salted water to a boil. Add asparagus; cook 3 minutes. Remove with slotted spoon; place in bowl with pesto. Return water to a boil. Add pasta; cook 2 to 3 minutes or until tender. Drain and add to bowl with pesto; toss gently to combine. Sprinkle with remaining ¼ cup Parmesan cheese.

Egg Pasta Dough

Makes about 1 pound

3 eggs

2 tablespoons water

1 tablespoon extra virgin olive oil

1 teaspoon salt

2¼ cups all-purpose flour

1 Attach flat beater to stand mixer; beat eggs, water, olive oil and salt in mixer bowl at low speed to combine. In three additions, add flour to make dough that clumps together. Stop mixer and press a few tablespoons of dough into small ball; dough should feel tacky, moist and pliable. If too wet, beat in flour, 1 tablespoon at a time. If too dry, beat in water, 1 tablespoon at a time. Gather dough into a ball.

2 Replace beater with dough hook; knead on low 5 minutes or until dough is smooth and elastic. Shape dough into a ball and wrap in plastic wrap; let rest at room temperature 20 minutes or refrigerate until ready to use.

3 Cut dough into quarters. Flatten one piece of dough; dust with flour. Rewrap remaining pieces to prevent drying out. Attach Pasta Sheet Roller to mixer and set to thickness setting 1. Turn mixer to medium speed; feed dough through rollers three or more times, folding and turning each time until smooth. If dough feels sticky, dust with flour. Change to setting 2 and feed dough sheet through rollers twice. Feed dough through once at settings 3 and 4; roll to suggested roller setting. Let dough sheets rest on floured surface 10 minutes. Replace roller with desired Pasta Cutter. Feed dough sheets through cutter.

SEMOLINA PASTA DOUGH: Substitute 1¼ cups semolina flour and 1 cup all-purpose flour for the 2¼ cups all-purpose flour.

Suggested Roller Settings

Setting	Uses
1 or 2	Kneading and thinning dough
3	Thick egg noodles
4 or 5	Lasagna noodles, fettuccine, spaghetti, ravioli
6 or 7	Tortellini, thin fettuccine, linguine
7 or 8	Angel hair (capellini)

Spinach Pasta Dough

Makes about 1¼ pounds

10 ounces fresh spinach*

3 eggs

1 tablespoon extra virgin olive oil

1 teaspoon salt

2¼ cups all-purpose flour

Or substitute 1 package (10 ounces) frozen chopped spinach, thawed, squeezed dry and very finely chopped. Proceed with step 2.

1 Rinse spinach and shake dry; place in large saucepan with water clinging to leaves. Cover and cook over medium heat 5 to 7 minutes or until wilted and tender, stirring occasionally. Rinse under cold water until cool; squeeze all excess liquid from spinach. Finely chop spinach and place in bowl of stand mixer.

2 Attach flat beater to stand mixer. Add eggs, olive oil and salt to spinach in mixer bowl; mix on low speed until blended. Gradually mix in flour until dough clumps together. Dough should feel tacky, moist and pliable. If too wet, mix in additional flour 1 tablespoon at a time. If too dry, add water 1 tablespoon at a time. Gather dough into a ball.

3 Replace flat beater with dough hook; knead on low speed 5 minutes or until smooth and elastic. Wrap dough ball in plastic wrap; let rest at room temperature 30 minutes or refrigerate until ready to use.

4 Cut dough into quarters. Flatten one piece of dough; dust with flour. Rewrap remaining pieces to prevent drying out. Remove dough hook; attach Pasta Sheet Roller to mixer and set to thickness setting 1. Turn mixer to medium speed; feed dough through rollers three or more times, folding and turning each time until smooth. If dough feels sticky, dust with flour. Change to setting 2 and feed dough sheet through rollers twice. Feed dough through once at settings 3 and 4; roll to desired thickness.

5 Let dough sheets rest on floured surface 10 minutes. Replace roller with desired Pasta Cutter. Feed dough sheets through cutter.

NOTE: Spinach needs to be very finely chopped or the dough will be hard to cut into noodles.

Whole Wheat Pasta Dough

Makes about 1 pound

2½ cups wheat berries *or* 3 cups whole wheat flour, sifted

2 eggs, beaten, plus water to equal ¾ cup

½ teaspoon salt

1 Attach Grain Mill to stand mixer. Place wheat berries in hopper and process on fine grind into bowl. Measure 3 cups flour and sift into mixer bowl. Remove Grain Mill; attach flat beater. Add egg mixture and salt to mixer bowl. Mix 30 seconds. Replace beater with dough hook; knead 1 to 2 minutes.

FOR PASTA PREPARED WITH ROLLER AND CUTTERS

2 Cut dough into eight pieces. Flatten one piece of dough; dust with flour. Rewrap remaining pieces to prevent drying out. Attach Pasta Sheet Roller to mixer and set to thickness setting 1. Turn mixer to medium speed; feed dough through rollers three or more times, folding and turning each time until smooth. If dough feels sticky, dust with flour. Change to setting 2 and feed dough sheet through rollers twice. Feed dough through once at settings 3 and 4; roll to suggested roller setting. Let dough sheets rest on floured surface 10 minutes. Replace roller with desired Pasta Cutter. Feed dough sheets through cutter.

FOR PASTA PREPARED WITH PASTA PRESS

3 Assemble Pasta Press with desired plate; attach to mixer. Feed walnut-sized pieces of dough into hopper and extrude pasta into desired shapes according to instruction book. Immediately separate pasta, dust with flour and spread in single layer on cloth or rack to dry 20 to 30 minutes.

Eggless Dough for Pasta Press

Makes about 1 pound

1½ cups all-purpose flour

1½ cups semolina flour

¾ cup water

1 Attach flat beater to stand mixer. Combine all-purpose flour and semolina flour in mixer bowl. Gradually add water on low. Stop when rough dough forms. Dough should stick together when pressed with fingers, but should be fairly dry. Add additional water by teaspoonfuls, if needed.

2 Assemble Pasta Press with desired pasta plate; attach to stand mixer. Feed walnut-size pieces of dough into hopper and extrude pasta to desired shape according to instruction book.

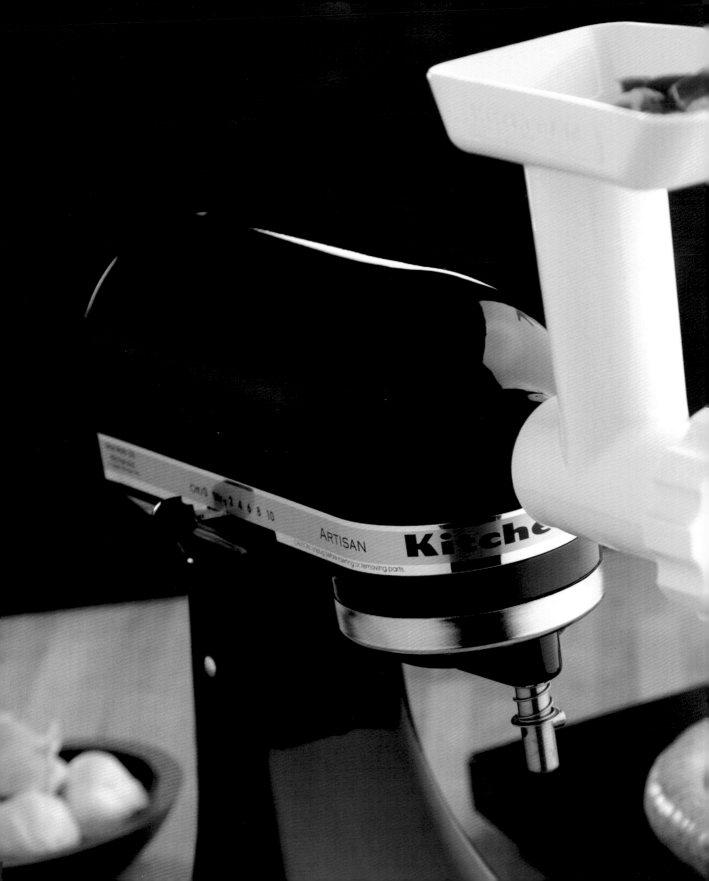

CHAPTER 5
ENTRÉES

Wasabi Flank Steak with Asian Slaw

Makes 4 servings

5 tablespoons rice vinegar, divided

2 tablespoons soy sauce

2 tablespoons dark sesame oil

1 tablespoon prepared wasabi paste

1 clove garlic, minced

1 piece peeled fresh ginger (about 1 inch), minced

1 flank steak (about 1¼ pounds)

1 small head napa cabbage, cut into wedges

5 radishes

1 carrot, peeled

4 green onions, finely chopped

3 tablespoons sugar

1½ teaspoons salt

1 Whisk 2 tablespoons vinegar, soy sauce, sesame oil, wasabi paste, garlic and ginger in small bowl. Place steak in large resealable food storage bag. Pour marinade over steak. Seal bag; turn to coat. Marinate in refrigerator at least 2 hours or overnight, turning occasionally.

2 For slaw, assemble Food Processor attachment with adjustable slicing disc; attach to stand mixer. Slide to third notch for medium slices. Slice cabbage through large feed tube into mixer bowl. Slide to first notch for thin slices. Slice radishes through feed tube into same bowl. Replace slicing disc with shredding disc with large holes facing up. Shred carrot into same bowl. Whisk green onion, remaining 3 tablespoons rice vinegar, sugar and salt in small bowl. Pour over vegetable mixture; toss to coat.

3 Drain steak; discard marinade. Pat steak dry. Heat large skillet over medium-high heat. Cook steak 4 to 6 minutes per side or to desired doneness. Transfer steak to cutting board; let rest 10 minutes before slicing. Carve steak against the grain into thin slices. Arrange slaw on serving plates; top with steak. Serve immediately.

Ultimate Grilled Burgers

Makes 4 servings

1½ pounds boneless beef chuck, excess fat trimmed, cut into 2-inch strips

1½ teaspoons kosher salt *or* 1¼ teaspoons regular salt

½ teaspoon freshly ground black pepper

Canola or olive oil

4 hamburger buns, split

Sliced tomatoes, lettuce leaves, red onion rings and pickle slices

Assorted condiments, such as ketchup, mayonnaise and mustard

1 Spread beef strips on baking sheet. Refrigerate or freeze until firm.

2 Assemble Food Grinder with coarse grinding plate; attach to stand mixer. Grind beef into mixer bowl. Mix in salt and pepper with clean hands. Do not overmix. Shape into four 4-inch patties, making 1-inch wide shallow indentation in center of each patty to discourage shrinkage. Cover with plastic wrap. Prepare grill for direct cooking.

3 Lightly brush patties with oil. Grill, covered, over high heat 2½ minutes or until browned on bottom. Turn and grill 2½ minutes or until cooked through (160°F). If flare-ups occur, move burgers away from flames. Grill buns, cut sides down, 1 minute or until toasted.

4 Serve burgers on buns with desired toppings and condiments.

Butternut Squash Ravioli with Sage Butter

Makes 4 servings

1 small butternut squash, halved and seeded

1 tablespoon olive oil

Pinch salt and freshly ground black pepper

1 cup ricotta cheese

¼ cup freshly grated Parmesan cheese, plus additional for serving

1 teaspoon ground nutmeg

1 recipe Ravioli Dough (page 89)

6 tablespoons salted butter

10 fresh sage leaves, coarsely chopped

1. Preheat oven to 400°F. Brush cut sides of squash with oil; sprinkle with salt and pepper. Place cut side down on baking sheet. Bake 45 minutes or until soft; let cool. Scoop out squash into medium bowl and mash (about 1 cup mashed squash). Stir in ricotta cheese, ¼ cup Parmesan cheese and nutmeg; set aside.

2. Meanwhile, prepare Ravioli Dough.

3. Attach Ravioli Maker to stand mixer. Fold one dough sheet in half. Fit folded end of dough between rollers and rotate handle one quarter turn just until rollers catch dough. Open loose ends of dough and drape over sides of Ravioli Maker.

4. Fit hopper into Ravioli Maker. Spread one spoonful of filling into hopper. Slowly turn handle, adding filling as needed. Place finished sheet of ravioli on clean cloth to dry 10 minutes. Repeat with remaining dough and filling.

5. Gently separate ravioli and trim edges. Keep ravioli in single layer to prevent sticking. Bring large pot of salted water to a boil. Add ravioli; cook 2 to 4 minutes or until barely tender. Remove with slotted spoon; keep warm.

6. Melt butter in large skillet over medium heat. Add sage; cook until butter begins to brown. Divide ravioli among serving plates; top with sage butter and additional Parmesan cheese.

Ravioli Dough

Makes about 1 pound

1¼ cups all-purpose flour

¾ cup semolina flour

3 eggs

1 tablespoon extra virgin olive oil

1 teaspoon salt

1 Attach flat beater to stand mixer. Combine all-purpose flour, semolina flour, eggs, olive oil and salt in mixer bowl; mix until dough comes together. Replace flat beater with dough hook; knead on low 2 to 3 minutes or until smooth and elastic. Wrap dough in plastic wrap; let rest 20 minutes or refrigerate until ready to use.

2 Cut dough into quarters. Flatten one piece of dough; dust with flour. Rewrap remaining pieces to prevent drying out. Attach Pasta Sheet Roller to mixer and set to thickness setting 1. Turn mixer to medium speed; feed dough through rollers three or more times, folding and turning each time until smooth. If dough feels sticky, dust with flour. Change to setting 2 and feed dough sheet through rollers twice making sure dough sheet is as wide as rollers.

3 Feed dough through once at settings 3, 4 and 5. Lay finished dough sheet on lightly floured surface. Repeat with remaining pieces of dough. (Let dough rest in single layer to prevent sticking.)

Pork and Parmesan Sausages

Makes about 3½ pounds sausage

3 pounds boneless pork shoulder, cut into 1½-inch strips

8 ounces sliced fresh (not salted or cured) pork fatback, cut into 1-inch pieces

¾ cup freshly grated Parmesan cheese

⅓ cup dry white wine, such as Pinot Grigio

3 tablespoons finely chopped fresh parsley

4 cloves garlic, finely chopped

1 tablespoon kosher salt *or* 2½ teaspoons regular salt

2 teaspoons dried oregano

¾ teaspoon freshly ground black pepper

⅛ teaspoon ground allspice

Sausage casings, soaked and drained*

See page 13.

1 Spread pork and fatback on baking sheet. Refrigerate or freeze until slightly firm. Assemble Food Grinder with coarse grinding plate; attach to stand mixer. Grind pork and fatback into mixer bowl.

2 Add Parmesan, wine, parsley, garlic, salt, oregano, pepper and allspice; mix well. Cover with plastic wrap and refrigerate 2 to 4 hours or until well chilled.

3 Reassemble Food Grinder with Sausage Stuffer; attach to mixer. Stuff casings with pork mixture. Refrigerate sausages, uncovered, at least 4 hours and up to 1 day to cure.

4 Grill, broil, or pan-fry sausages until cooked through (160°F). Serve hot.

Marvelous Meat Loaf

Makes 6 to 8 servings

1½ pounds boneless beef chuck, excess fat trimmed, cut into 1½-inch chunks

6 ounces stale French bread

½ pound spicy bulk pork breakfast sausage

½ cup shredded carrots

½ onion

2 eggs

¾ cup ketchup, divided

3 teaspoons chili powder, divided

¾ teaspoon salt

1 Spread beef chunks on baking sheet. Freeze until slightly firm, about 1 hour.

2 Preheat oven to 375°F. Assemble Food Grinder with coarse grinding plate. Grind bread into mixer bowl; measure ¾ cup and set aside. Grind beef into same bowl. Remove Food Grinder; attach Food Processor fitted with shredding disc. Shred carrots into same bowl. Replace shredding disc with dicing disc; dice onion into same bowl. Remove Food Processor; attach flat beater. Add sausage, bread crumbs, eggs, ¼ cup ketchup, 2 teaspoons chili powder and salt to bowl; mix on low speed until well blended. Press into 9×5-inch loaf pan.

3 Combine remaining ½ cup ketchup and 1 teaspoon chili powder in small bowl; spread over top of loaf.

4 Bake 1 hour or until internal temperature of loaf reaches 165°F. Let stand 5 minutes before slicing.

Pastitsio

Makes 6 servings

½ recipe Eggless Dough for Pasta Press (page 81), cut into small macaroni

½ onion

4 ounces Parmesan cheese

1 pound ground lamb or beef

1 clove garlic, minced

1 can (8 ounces) tomato sauce

½ teaspoon dried oregano

½ teaspoon freshly ground black pepper

¼ teaspoon ground cinnamon

2 tablespoons butter

2 tablespoons all-purpose flour

1½ cups milk

1 egg

1 Prepare pasta with Pasta Press.

2 Preheat oven to 350°F. Grease 9-inch baking dish. Bring large pot of salted water to a boil; cook pasta 2 to 3 minutes or until al dente. Drain; keep warm.

3 Assemble Food Processor with dicing disc; attach to stand mixer. Dice onion into small bowl. Replace dicing disc with shredding disc; shred Parmesan cheese into separate small bowl.

4 Brown lamb in large nonstick skillet over medium-high heat 6 to 8 minutes, stirring to break up meat. Drain all but 1 tablespoon fat. Add onion; sauté 2 minutes or until translucent. Add garlic; sauté 30 seconds. Stir in tomato sauce, oregano, pepper and cinnamon. Reduce heat to low; simmer 10 minutes.

5 Spread half of pasta in prepared dish. Top with lamb mixture, then remaining pasta.

6 For sauce, melt butter in medium saucepan over medium-low heat. Whisk in flour. Cook 1 minute, whisking constantly. Whisk in milk. Cook 6 minutes or until thickened, whisking frequently. Beat egg in small bowl; stir in some of sauce. Pour egg mixture into saucepan; cook 2 minutes, whisking frequently. Remove from heat; stir in ¾ cup Parmesan cheese until smooth.

7 Pour sauce over pasta in baking dish. Sprinkle with remaining Parmesan cheese. Bake 30 minutes or until heated through and golden brown.

Asparagus, Chicken and Goat Cheese Pizza

Makes 4 servings

New York-Style Pizza Crust (recipe follows)

1 jar (10 ounces) roasted red bell peppers

½ teaspoon whole fennel seeds, crushed

6 ounces boneless skinless chicken breast, thinly sliced crosswise

3 tablespoons chopped sun-dried tomatoes (not oil-packed)

10 to 12 spears fresh asparagus, trimmed

6 tablespoons (3 ounces) feta cheese *or* 6 ounces soft goat cheese, crumbled

1 Prepare New York-Style Pizza Crust. While crust rises, prepare toppings. Place roasted peppers in blender with fennel; process until smooth. Set aside.

2 Bring 1 quart water to a boil in medium saucepan. Add chicken strips; cover and remove from heat. Let stand 6 to 8 minutes or until no longer pink in center; drain. Place sun-dried tomatoes in small bowl; cover with hot water. Let stand 10 to 15 minutes or until soft; drain.

3 Place asparagus spears on microwavable plate. Cover and microwave on HIGH 2½ minutes or until tender. Cut into 2-inch pieces when cool enough to handle.

4 Preheat oven to 500°F. Bake crust 3 to 4 minutes or until top is crisp and beginning to brown. Spread roasted pepper sauce over pizza crust to within ½ inch of edge. Layer with chicken, asparagus, tomatoes and cheese.

5 Bake 12 to 15 minutes or until crust is golden and crisp on bottom and cheese is golden.

New York-Style Pizza Crust

1¾ cups all-purpose or bread flour

1 teaspoon sugar

1 teaspoon active dry yeast

½ teaspoon salt

⅔ cup warm water (120°F)

1 Attach dough hook to stand mixer. Combine flour, sugar, yeast and salt in mixer bowl; stir in water until soft dough forms. Knead on low speed 5 minutes or until dough is smooth and elastic, adding additional flour, 1 tablespoon at a time, if needed. Place dough in large lightly greased medium bowl; turn once to grease surface. Cover and let rise in warm place about 30 minutes or until doubled.

2 Punch down dough; knead on lightly floured surface 2 minutes or until smooth. Pat dough into flat disc. Let rest 2 to 3 minutes.

3 Pat and gently stretch dough into large thin circle, allowing it to rest for a few minutes if it becomes hard to stretch. Transfer to greased baking sheet or pizza pan.

Makes dough for 1 pizza

Cubano Burgers

Makes 4 servings

1½ pounds boneless pork shoulder, cut into 1½ inch strips

¼ cup minced green onions

3 tablespoons yellow mustard, divided

1 tablespoon minced garlic

2 teaspoons paprika

½ teaspoon freshly ground black pepper

¼ teaspoon salt

8 slices Swiss cheese

4 bolillos or Kaiser rolls, split and toasted

8 slices sandwich-style dill pickles

¼ pound thinly sliced ham

1 Spread pork on baking sheet. Refrigerate or freeze until slightly firm. Assemble Food Grinder with coarse grinding plate; attach to stand mixer. Grind pork into mixer bowl.

2 Add green onions, 1 tablespoon mustard, garlic, paprika, pepper and salt; mix lightly but thoroughly. Shape into four patties about ¾ inch thick, shaping to fit rolls.

3 Prepare grill for direct cooking.

4 Place patties on grid over medium heat. Grill, covered, 8 to 10 minutes (or uncovered, 13 to 15 minutes) until cooked through (160°F), turning occasionally. Top each burger with 2 slices Swiss cheese during last 2 minutes of grilling.

5 Spread remaining 2 tablespoons mustard over cut sides of rolls. Place pickles on bottom half of each roll. Top each with burger and ham. Cover with top halves of rolls.

Italian Sausage

See page 13.

Makes 3 pounds sausage

3 pounds boneless pork shoulder, cut into 1½-inch strips

3 teaspoons salt

1½ teaspoons freshly ground black pepper

1¼ teaspoons ground red pepper

2 cloves garlic, minced

1 teaspoon onion powder

1 teaspoon ground paprika

⅛ teaspoon dried marjoram

⅛ teaspoon dried rosemary

⅛ teaspoon dried thyme

½ cup dry red wine

1 tablespoon shortening

Sausage casings, soaked and drained*

1 Spread pork on baking sheet. Refrigerate or freeze until slightly firm.

2 Combine salt, black pepper, red pepper, garlic, onion powder, paprika, marjoram, rosemary and thyme in small bowl. Sprinkle mixture over pork; toss to coat evenly.

3 Assemble Food Grinder with coarse grinding plate; attach to stand mixer. Grind pork into mixer bowl. Spread pork on same baking sheet; freeze until very cold.

4 Place pork in mixer bowl; add wine and stir until well blended.

5 Reassemble Food Grinder with Sausage Stuffer; attach to mixer. Stuff casings with pork mixture. Refrigerate sausages until ready to cook.

6 Grill, broil, or pan-fry sausages until cooked through (160°F). Serve hot.

Tofu Carrot Curry

Makes 4 servings

1 pound carrots

2 medium sweet potatoes
(about ¾ pound),
peeled

1 apple, quartered and
seeded

1 clove garlic

1 piece (1 inch) fresh ginger

2 teaspoons extra virgin
olive oil

1 tablespoon Thai red
curry paste

3 cups vegetable broth

1 cup light coconut milk

1 tablespoon fresh lime
juice

1 tablespoon soy sauce

1 package (14 ounces)
firm or extra firm tofu,
drained cut into cubes

1 Assemble Juicer and Sauce attachment with low pulp screen; attach to stand mixer. Juice carrots, sweet potatoes, apple, garlic and ginger. Measure 1 cup.

2 Heat olive oil in medium saucepan over medium heat. Add curry paste; cook and stir 1 minute or until fragrant. Add juice and vegetable broth; bring to a simmer. Stir in coconut milk, lime juice and soy sauce. Add tofu cubes and cook until heated through. Serve warm.

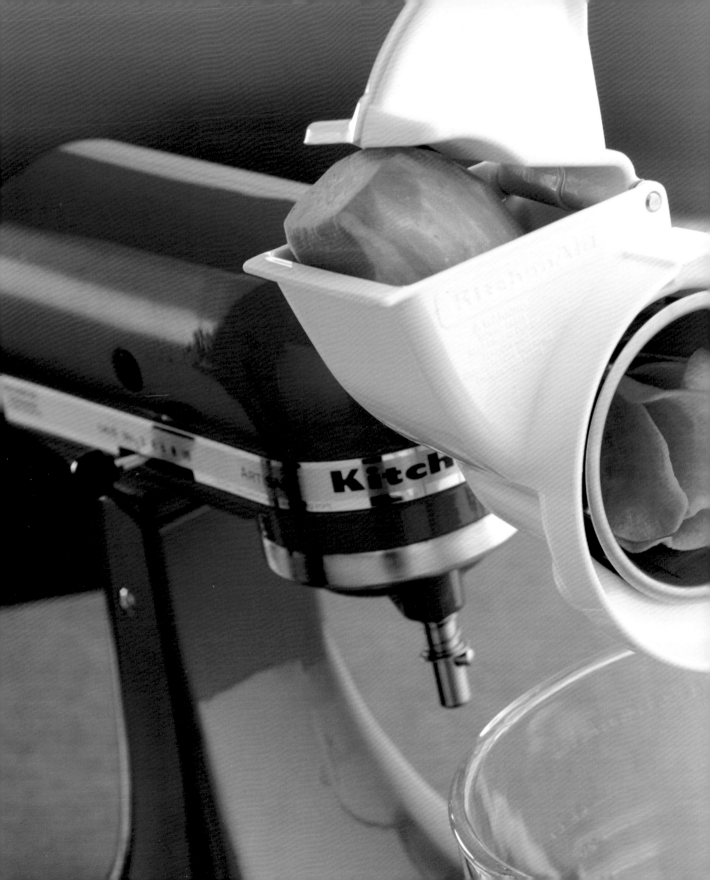

CHAPTER 6
SIDE DISHES

Tomato-Mango Ketchup

Makes ¾ cup ketchup

1 pound plum tomatoes, halved *or* 1 can (14 ounces) whole Italian plum tomatoes, undrained

1 mango, pitted and peeled

½ medium onion

1 clove garlic

3 tablespoons white vinegar

2 tablespoons sugar

1 tablespoon tomato paste

Salt and freshly ground black pepper

1 Assemble Juicer and Sauce attachment with sauce screen (pulp control closed). Juice tomatoes, mango, onion and garlic. (If using canned tomatoes, reserve juice and add to saucepan in step 2).

2 Combine juice, vinegar, sugar and tomato paste in medium saucepan. Bring to a boil over medium-high heat. Reduce heat to low; simmer 30 to 40 minutes or until mixture is significantly reduced and thickened to desired consistency. Season to taste with salt and pepper. Cool completely. Store leftovers in an airtight jar or container in the refrigerator 1 to 2 weeks.

NOTE: For smoother ketchup, process cooled tomato mixture in a food processor until desired consistency is reached.

Sesame Miso Cucumber Salad

Makes 10 servings

2   medium cucumbers, ends trimmed

2   green onions, sliced

2   tablespoons yellow miso*

1½ tablespoons rice vinegar

1½ tablespoons honey

1   tablespoon hot water

1   tablespoon dark sesame oil

1   teaspoon red pepper flakes

1   teaspoon chopped fresh ginger

¼   teaspoon coarse salt

1½ tablespoons toasted sesame seeds

*If miso is not available, substitute 1½ tablespoons soy sauce and 1 teaspoon lime juice.

1   Assemble Food Processor attachment with dicing disc; attach to stand mixer. Dice cucumbers into large bowl. Stir in green onions.

2   Remove Food Processor; attach wire whip. Combine miso, vinegar, honey, hot water, sesame oil, red pepper flakes, ginger and salt in mixer bowl. Whip on medium-high speed 30 seconds to 1 minute or until well blended. Add to cucumber mixture; stir gently to coat. Serve immediately or refrigerate up to 1 hour. Sprinkle with sesame seeds just before serving.

Oven-Roasted Onion Soup

Makes 4 servings

3 yellow onions, halved

4 ounces Swiss cheese, partially frozen

¼ cup (½ stick) butter

1 teaspoon salt

½ teaspoon freshly ground black pepper

6 cups reduced-sodium beef broth

½ cup brewed coffee

¼ cup dry sherry

1 small baguette, cut into 8 (½-inch) slices

6 small sprigs fresh thyme (optional)

1 Preheat oven to 325°F. Assemble Rotor Slicer/Shredder with thick slicing cone; attach to stand mixer. Slice onions into mixer bowl. Replace thick slicing cone with coarse shredding cone; shred cheese into medium bowl. Cover and refrigerate.

2 Melt butter in Dutch oven over medium heat. Add onions, salt and pepper. Cook and stir 10 minutes or until onions are golden but not browned. Cover and bake 45 minutes, stirring once.

3 Stir in broth; cover and bake 30 minutes. Remove from oven; stir in coffee and sherry. Bring to a simmer over medium heat. Remove from heat.

4 Place bread slices on baking sheet. Bake until lightly browned on both sides, turning once.

5 Preheat broiler. Place four ovenproof bowls in large baking pan. Ladle soup evenly into bowls. Top each serving with two slices of toast and 1 tablespoon Swiss cheese.

6 Broil 2 to 3 minutes or until cheese is melted and bubbly. Garnish with thyme.

Spiced Apple-Pear Sauce

Makes 4 cups sauce

1 pound pears, cored and quartered

2 to 2½ pounds apples, peeled, cored and quartered

¼ cup packed brown sugar

1 teaspoon ground cinnamon

½ teaspoon ground nutmeg

¼ teaspoon ground cloves

1 Assemble Juicer and Sauce attachment with saucing screen (pulp control closed); attach to stand mixer. Juice pears and enough apples to yield 4 cups of pulp. Combine pulp, brown sugar, cinnamon, nutmeg and cloves in medium saucepan. Simmer over medium-low heat until thickened to desired consistency.

2 Cool to room temperature. Store leftover sauce in an airtight jar or container in the refrigerator 2 to 3 weeks.

Beet and Blue Cheese Salad

Makes 4 servings

½ red onion, cut in half

2 carrots, peeled

1 package (6 ounces) baby spinach

1 cup sliced cooked beets

¼ cup balsamic vinegar

2 tablespoons canola oil

2 tablespoons maple syrup

¼ teaspoon salt

⅛ teaspoon red pepper flakes

¼ cup crumbled blue cheese

1 Assemble Food Processor attachment with dicing kit; attach to stand mixer. Dice onion into medium bowl. Replace dicing kit with julienne disc; julienne carrots into same bowl.

2 Divide spinach among four plates. Top evenly with beets, onion and carrots.

3 Remove Food Processor; attach wire whip. Whip vinegar, oil, maple syrup, salt and red pepper flakes in mixer bowl on medium speed until smooth and well blended. Drizzle dressing over salad. Sprinkle evenly with blue cheese.

Cheddar and Leek Strata

Makes 12 servings

2 small leeks, ends trimmed

1 red bell pepper, halved

6 ounces Swiss cheese, partially frozen

6 ounces sharp Cheddar cheese, partially frozen

8 eggs

2 cups milk

½ cup porter or stout

2 cloves garlic, minced

¼ teaspoon salt

¼ teaspoon freshly ground black pepper

1 loaf (16 ounces) sourdough bread, cut into ½-inch cubes

1 Assemble Food Processor attachment with dicing disc; attach to stand mixer. Dice leeks and bell pepper into large bowl; mix well. Replace dicing disc with shredding disc; shred cheeses into large bowl. Mix well.

2 Remove Food Processor; attach wire whip. Whip eggs, milk, porter, garlic, salt and black pepper in mixer bowl on medium speed until well blended.

3 Spray 13×9-inch baking dish with nonstick cooking spray. Spread half of bread cubes in prepared baking dish. Sprinkle with half of vegetable mixture. Top with 1½ cups cheese. Repeat layers. Pour egg mixture evenly over top.

4 Cover tightly with plastic wrap or foil. Weigh top of strata down with slightly smaller baking dish. Refrigerate at least 2 hours or overnight.

5 Preheat oven to 350°F. Bake, uncovered, 40 to 45 minutes or until center is set. Serve immediately.

Pesto Potato Salad

Makes 6 to 8 servings

1½ pounds small waxy
  potatoes, such as
  fingerling or Yukon
  Gold

½ medium red onion *or*
  2 small shallots

4 stalks celery

1½ teaspoons salt, divided

1½ cups fresh arugula,
  divided

2 ounces Parmesan cheese,
  finely chopped

¼ cup toasted pine nuts,*
  finely chopped

3 tablespoons water

2 tablespoons extra virgin
  olive oil

1 clove garlic, minced

**To toast pine nuts, spread in single
layer in heavy skillet. Cook over
medium-low heat 2 minutes or until
nuts are lightly browned and fragrant,
stirring frequently.*

1 Assemble Food Processor attachment with adjustable slicing disc; attach to stand mixer. Slide to sixth notch for thick slices. Slice potatoes into rounds into large bowl. Transfer potatoes to large saucepan. Slide to first notch for thin slices. Slice onion into same bowl. Slide to third notch for medium slices. Slice celery into same bowl.

2 Cover potatoes with water and add 1 teaspoon salt. Bring to a simmer over medium-high heat; cook 10 to 12 minutes or until potatoes are fork-tender. Drain potatoes; refrigerate until cold.

3 Meanwhile for pesto, remove Food Processor; attach flat beater. Finely chop ¾ cup arugula; place in mixer bowl. Add cheese, pine nuts, 3 tablespoons water, olive oil, garlic and remaining ½ teaspoon salt. Mix on medium speed about 1 minute or until pesto is creamy.

4 Add potatoes to bowl with onions and celery. Add remaining ¾ cup arugula; toss to combine. Add pesto; toss gently to coat. Serve immediately or refrigerate until ready to serve.

CHAPTER 7
BREADS

Cinnamon Raisin Bread

Makes 1 loaf

1 cup milk

3 tablespoons butter

3 to 3½ cups all-purpose flour, divided

½ cup sugar, divided

1 package (¼ ounce) active dry yeast (2¼ teaspoons)

1 teaspoon salt

1 whole egg

1 egg, separated

1 teaspoon vanilla

¾ cup raisins

1 tablespoon ground cinnamon

1 tablespoon butter, melted

1 tablespoon water

1 Combine milk and 3 tablespoons butter in small saucepan; heat over low heat to 115° to 120°F (butter does not need to melt completely).

2 Attach flat beater to stand mixer. Whisk 1½ cups flour, ¼ cup sugar, yeast and salt in mixer bowl. Gradually add milk mixture on low speed until blended. Beat on medium speed 2 minutes. Add whole egg, egg yolk and vanilla; beat 2 minutes. Beat in enough additional flour, about 1½ cups, to make soft dough.

3 Replace flat beater with dough hook; knead on low speed about 5 minutes or until dough is smooth and elastic. Add enough remaining flour, 1 tablespoon at a time, if necessary to clean side of bowl. Add raisins; knead on low until incorporated. (Dough will be soft and sticky.) Knead several times on lightly floured surface; shape dough into a ball. Place dough in large lightly greased bowl; turn to grease top. Cover and let rise in warm place about 1 hour or until doubled.

4 Turn out dough onto lightly floured surface; knead 1 minute. Cover and let rest 10 minutes. Grease 9×5-inch loaf pan. Combine remaining ¼ cup sugar and cinnamon in small bowl; reserve 1 teaspoon mixture for top of loaf, if desired.

5 Roll dough into 20×9-inch rectangle. Brush with 1 tablespoon melted butter; sprinkle with cinnamon-sugar. Starting with short side, tightly roll up dough. Pinch ends and seam to seal. Place loaf seam side down in prepared pan; cover and let rise in warm place about 30 minutes or until doubled.

6 Preheat oven to 375°F. Beat egg white and water in small bowl. Brush over top of loaf; sprinkle with reserved cinnamon-sugar.

7 Bake 40 to 45 minutes or until loaf sounds hollow when tapped and internal temperature reaches 190°F. Cover loosely with foil halfway through baking time if loaf is browning too fast. Immediately remove from pan; cool completely on wire rack.

Oatmeal Honey Bread

Makes 1 loaf

½ cup wheat berries *or* ½ cup whole wheat flour

1⅓ cups plus 1 tablespoon water, divided

¼ cup honey

2 tablespoons butter

1½ to 2 cups all-purpose flour

1 cup plus 1 tablespoon old-fashioned oats, divided

1 package (¼ ounce) active dry yeast (2¼ teaspoons)

1 teaspoon salt

1 egg

1 Attach Grain Mill to stand mixer. Place wheat berries in hopper; process on fine grind into bowl. Measure ½ cup.*

2 Heat 1⅓ cups water, honey and butter in small saucepan over low heat until honey dissolves and butter melts. Let cool to 130°F.

3 Remove Grain Mill; attach flat beater. Combine 1½ cups all-purpose flour, 1 cup oats, ½ cup whole wheat flour, yeast and salt in mixer bowl. Add water mixture; beat on medium speed 2 minutes. Add additional all-purpose flour by tablespoonfuls until dough begins to cling together. Dough should be shaggy and very sticky, not dry. (Dough should not form a ball and/or clean side of bowl.)

4 Replace flat beater with dough hook; knead on low speed 4 minutes. Transfer dough to large lightly greased bowl; turn to grease top. Cover and let rise in warm place about 45 minutes or until doubled.

5 Spray 8×4-inch loaf pan with nonstick cooking spray. Punch down dough; turn out onto floured surface. Flatten and stretch dough into 8-inch-long oval. Bring long sides together and pinch to seal; fold over short ends and pinch to seal. Place dough seam side down in prepared pan. Cover and let rise in warm place 20 to 30 minutes or until dough reaches top of pan.

6 Preheat oven to 375°F. Beat egg and remaining 1 tablespoon water in small bowl. Brush top of loaf with egg mixture; sprinkle with remaining 1 tablespoon oats.

7 Bake 30 to 35 minutes or until bread sounds hollow when tapped (about 190°F). Cool in pan 10 minutes; remove to wire rack to cool completely.

Store leftover flour in the refrigerator or freezer for another use.

Treacle Bread (Brown Soda Bread)

Makes 1 loaf

⅔ cup wheat berries *or* 1 cup whole wheat flour

2 cups all-purpose flour

1 teaspoon baking soda

½ teaspoon salt

½ teaspoon ground ginger

1¼ cups buttermilk, plus additional as needed

3 tablespoons molasses (preferably blackstrap)

1 Attach Grain Mill to stand mixer. Place wheat berries in hopper; process on fine grind into bowl. Measure 1 cup.*

2 Preheat oven to 375°F. Line baking sheet with parchment paper.

3 Remove Grain Mill; attach flat beater. Combine all-purpose flour, 1 cup whole wheat flour, baking soda, salt and ginger in mixer bowl; mix on low speed until blended.

4 Combine 1¼ cups buttermilk and molasses in small bowl; mix well. Add to flour mixture; mix on low until dry, rough dough forms, adding additional buttermilk by tablespoonfuls if needed.

5 Turn out dough onto floured surface; knead 8 to 10 times or just until smooth. (Do not overknead.) Shape dough into round loaf about 1½ inches thick. Place on prepared baking sheet.

6 Use floured knife to cut halfway through dough, scoring into quarters (called farls in Ireland). Sprinkle top of dough with additional flour, if desired.

7 Bake about 35 minutes or until bread sounds hollow when tapped. Remove to wire rack to cool slightly. Serve warm.

NOTE: Treacle Bread can be sliced or pulled apart into farls.

Store leftover flour in the refrigerator or freezer for another use.

Prosciutto Provolone Rolls

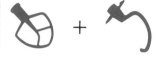

Makes 12 rolls

3 cups all-purpose flour, divided

1 package (¼ ounce) active dry yeast (2¼ teaspoons)

1¼ teaspoons salt

1 cup warm water (120°F)

2 tablespoons olive oil

⅓ cup garlic and herb spreadable cheese

6 thin slices prosciutto (3-ounce package)

6 slices (1 ounce each) provolone cheese

1 Attach flat beater to stand mixer. Combine 1½ cups flour, yeast and salt in mixer bowl; mix on low speed 10 seconds. Add water and oil; mix on low speed until soft dough forms.

2 Replace flat beater with dough hook. Add remaining 1½ cups flour; knead on low speed 5 to 7 minutes or until dough is smooth and elastic.

3 Shape dough into a ball. Place dough in large lightly greased bowl; turn once to grease surface. Cover and let rise in warm place about 30 minutes or until doubled.

4 Spray 12 standard (2½-inch) muffin cups with nonstick cooking spray. Punch down dough. Roll out dough into 12×10-inch rectangle on lightly floured surface.

5 Spread garlic and herb cheese evenly over dough. Arrange prosciutto slices over herb cheese; top with provolone slices. Starting with long side, tightly roll up dough; pinch seam to seal. Cut crosswise into 1-inch slices; arrange slices cut sides up in prepared muffin cups. Cover and let rise in warm place about 25 minutes or until almost doubled. Preheat oven to 375°F.

6 Bake about 20 minutes or until golden brown. Loosen edges of rolls with knife; remove to wire rack. Serve warm.

Three-Grain Bread

Makes 1 loaf

⅔ cup wheat berries *or* 1 cup whole wheat flour

1 cup milk

2 tablespoons honey

1 tablespoon olive oil

1 teaspoon salt

¾ cup all-purpose flour

1 package (¼ ounce) active dry yeast (2¼ teaspoons)

½ cup plus 1 tablespoon old-fashioned oats, divided

¼ cup whole grain cornmeal, plus additional for baking sheet

1 egg beaten with 1 tablespoon water (optional)

1 Attach Grain Mill to stand mixer. Place wheat berries in hopper; process on fine grind into bowl. Measure 1 cup.*

2 Heat milk, honey, olive oil and salt in small saucepan over low heat until warm (115° to 120°F).

3 Remove Grain Mill; attach flat beater. Combine 1 cup whole wheat flour, all-purpose flour and yeast in mixer bowl. Stir in milk mixture on low speed. Increase speed to high; beat 3 minutes. Gradually add ½ cup oats and ¼ cup cornmeal on low speed. If dough is too wet, add additional flour by teaspoonfuls until it begins to come together.

4 Replace flat beater with dough hook; knead on low speed 5 to 7 minutes or until dough forms a ball. Place dough in large lightly greased bowl; turn once to grease surface. Cover and let rise warm place about 1 hour or until dough is puffy and does not spring back when touched.

5 Sprinkle baking sheet with cornmeal. Punch dough down and shape into 8-inch long loaf. Place on prepared baking sheet. Cover and let rise in warm place 45 minutes or until almost doubled. Preheat oven to 375°F.

6 Make shallow slash down center of loaf with sharp knife. Brush lightly with egg mixture, if desired, and sprinkle with remaining 1 tablespoon oats.

7 Bake 30 minutes or until loaf sounds hollow when tapped (about 200°F). Remove to wire rack; cool completely.

Store leftover flour in the refrigerator or freezer for another use.

Focaccia

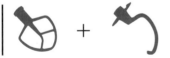

Makes 12 servings

4 cups all-purpose flour, divided

1 package (¼ ounce) active dry yeast (2¼ teaspoons)

1 teaspoon sugar

1 teaspoon salt

1½ cups warm water (120°F)

7 tablespoons olive oil, divided

¼ cup bottled roasted red peppers, drained and cut into strips

¼ cup pitted black olives

1 Attach flat beater to stand mixer. Combine 3 cups flour, yeast, sugar and salt in mixer bowl; mix on low speed 10 seconds. Add water and 3 tablespoons oil; mix on low speed until soft dough forms.

2 Replace flat beater with dough hook. Add remaining 1 cup flour; knead on low speed 5 to 7 minutes or until dough is smooth and elastic.

3 Shape dough into a ball. Place dough in large lightly greased bowl; turn once to grease surface. Cover and let rise in warm place about 1 hour or until doubled.

4 Brush 15×10-inch jelly-roll pan with 1 tablespoon oil. Punch down dough. Turn out dough onto lightly floured surface. Flatten into rectangle; roll out almost to size of pan. Place dough in pan; gently press dough to edges.

5 Poke surface of dough with end of wooden spoon handle, making indentations every 1 or 2 inches. Brush with remaining 3 tablespoons oil. Gently press peppers and olives into dough. Cover and let rise in warm place about 30 minutes or until doubled. Preheat oven to 450°F.

6 Bake 12 to 18 minutes or until golden brown. Cut into squares. Serve warm.

Pull-Apart Rye Rolls

Makes 24 rolls

½ cup rye berries or rye flour

1 cup milk

2 tablespoons butter, softened

2 tablespoons molasses

2¼ cups all-purpose flour, divided

1 package (¼ ounce) active dry yeast (2¼ teaspoons)

1½ teaspoons salt

1½ teaspoons caraway seeds

Melted butter

1 Attach Grain Mill to stand mixer. Place rye berries in hopper; process on fine grind into bowl. Measure ½ cup.*

2 Heat milk, softened butter and molasses in small saucepan over low heat until temperature reaches 120°F (butter does not need to melt completely).

3 Remove Grain Mill; attach flat beater. Combine 1¼ cups all-purpose flour, rye flour, yeast, salt and caraway seeds in mixer bowl; mix on low speed 10 seconds. Add milk mixture; mix on low speed until soft, sticky dough forms. Gradually add additional all-purpose flour by tablespoons until rough dough forms.

4 Replace flat beater with dough hook; knead 5 to 7 minutes or until dough is smooth and elastic, adding remaining all-purpose flour by tablespoonfuls to prevent sticking if necessary. Shape dough into a ball. Place dough in large lightly greased bowl; turn once to grease surface. Cover and let rise in warm place about 30 minutes or until almost doubled.

5 Grease 8- or 9-inch round baking pan. Turn out dough onto lightly floured surface; divide in half. Roll each half into 12-inch log. Using sharp knife, cut each log into 12 pieces; shape into balls. Arrange in prepared pan. Brush tops with melted butter. Loosely cover with greased plastic wrap. Let rise in warm place about 45 minutes or until doubled.

6 Preheat oven to 375°F. Uncover rolls; bake 15 to 20 minutes or until golden brown. Cool in pan on wire rack 5 minutes. Remove to wire rack; cool completely.

Store leftover flour in the refrigerator or freezer for another use.

Gannat (French Cheese Bread)

Makes 1 loaf

2½ cups all-purpose flour

1 package (¼ ounce) active dry yeast (2¼ teaspoons)

1 teaspoon sugar

1 teaspoon salt

¼ cup (½ stick) butter, softened

2 eggs, beaten

4 to 6 tablespoons warm water (120°F)

4 ounces Emmentaler Swiss, Gruyère, sharp Cheddar or Swiss cheese

1 teaspoon vegetable oil

1 Attach flat beater to stand mixer. Combine flour, yeast, sugar and salt in mixer bowl; mix on low until blended. Add butter, eggs and 4 tablespoons water; mix on low until soft dough forms. Add additional water by tablespoonfuls if dough is too dry.

2 Replace flat beater with dough hook; knead on low 5 to 7 minutes or until dough is smooth and elastic. Shape dough into a ball. Place dough in large lightly greased bowl; turn once to grease surface. Cover and let rise in warm place about 1 hour or until doubled.

3 Assemble Rotor Slicer/Shredder with coarse shredding cone; attach to mixer. Shred cheese into bowl.

4 Grease 9-inch round baking pan. Turn out dough onto lightly greased surface; knead all but 2 tablespoons cheese into dough. Roll or pat into 8-inch circle. Place in prepared pan. Brush with oil; sprinkle with reserved cheese. Let stand in warm place about 45 minutes or until doubled. Preheat oven to 375°F.

5 Bake 30 to 35 minutes or until browned and bread sounds hollow when tapped. Immediately remove from pan; cool on wire rack.

New York Rye Bread

Makes 2 loaves

2 cups rye berries or rye flour

⅔ cup wheat berries *or* 1 cup whole wheat flour

2 cups warm water (120°F)

⅓ cup packed brown sugar

2 tablespoons vegetable oil

1 tablespoon salt

1 package (¼ ounce) active dry yeast (2¼ teaspoons)

3 to 3½ cups bread flour, divided

1 tablespoon caraway seeds

1 teaspoon cornmeal

1 Attach Grain Mill to stand mixer. Place rye berries in hopper; process on fine grind into large bowl. Measure 2 cups.* Place wheat berries in hopper; process on fine grind into separate bowl. Measure 1 cup; place in medium bowl and stir in 2 cups rye flour.

2 Remove Grain Mill; attach flat beater. Combine warm water, brown sugar, oil, salt and yeast in mixer bowl; mix on low speed until yeast is dissolved. Add 2 cups bread flour; mix on low speed 2 minutes. Gradually mix in rye flour mixture, caraway seeds and enough remaining bread flour to form soft dough.

3 Replace flat beater with dough hook; knead on low speed 7 to 10 minutes or until dough is smooth and elastic. Shape dough into a ball. Place dough in large lightly greased bowl; turn once to grease surface. Cover and let rise in warm place 1½ to 2 hours or until doubled.

4 Grease large baking sheet; sprinkle with cornmeal. Turn out dough onto lightly floured surface; divide in half. Shape each half into 10-inch-long oblong loaf; place on prepared baking sheet. Cover and let rise in warm place about 45 minutes or until almost doubled.

5 Preheat oven to 375°F. Spray or brush loaf with cool water; sprinkle lightly with bread flour. Cut three ¼-inch-deep slashes on top of loaves with sharp serrated knife.

6 Bake 25 to 30 minutes or until loaves sound hollow when tapped. Remove to wire rack; cool completely.

Store leftover flour in the refrigerator or freezer for another use.

CHAPTER 8
CAKES AND PIES

Sage Cake with Herbed Strawberries

Makes 12 servings

⅔ cup milk

14 whole fresh sage leaves, divided

1 pound fresh strawberries, hulled

1 tablespoon fresh thyme, chopped

1 cup plus 1 tablespoon sugar, divided

1 teaspoon red wine vinegar

⅛ teaspoon freshly ground black pepper

4 egg yolks

1 teaspoon vanilla

2 cups cake flour, sifted

1 tablespoon baking powder

½ teaspoon salt

½ cup (1 stick) butter, cut into small pieces, softened

1 Place milk in small saucepan. Crush or twist 6 sage leaves and tear them in half; add to milk. Heat over medium-low heat until bubbles form around edge of pan. Set aside to steep 15 minutes. Refrigerate until milk is cold. Strain milk through fine-mesh strainer.

2 Assemble Food Processor attachment with adjustable slicing disc; attach to stand mixer. Slide to third notch for medium slices. Slice strawberries horizontally into medium bowl. Stir in thyme, 1 tablespoon sugar, vinegar and pepper. Let stand at room temperature at least 30 minutes or refrigerate up to 24 hours.

3 Preheat oven to 350°F. Grease and flour 9-inch cake pan.

4 Remove Food Processor; attach flat beater. Combine ⅓ cup milk, egg yolks and vanilla in small bowl. Combine cake flour, remaining 1 cup sugar, baking powder and salt in mixer bowl; mix on low speed 10 seconds. Gradually add butter a few pieces at a time on low speed. Add remaining ⅓ cup milk until ingredients are moistened. Gradually beat in egg mixture on low speed. Increase speed to medium; beat 1 minute until light and fluffy.

5 Pour batter into prepared pan and arrange remaining sage leaves on top of batter.

6 Bake 28 to 30 minutes or until toothpick inserted into center comes out clean and edge of cake starts to pull away from side of pan. Cool in pan on rack 10 minutes; remove to wire rack. Invert onto serving plate. Serve warm with strawberries.

Classic White Cake

Makes 12 servings

Lemon Curd (page 19)

2¼ cups cake flour

1 tablespoon baking powder

½ teaspoon salt

1½ cups sugar

½ cup (1 stick) butter, softened

4 egg whites

2 teaspoons vanilla

1 cup milk

Buttercream Frosting (recipe follows)

Strawberry Filling (page 137)

Fresh strawberries (optional)

1 Prepare Lemon Curd.

2 Preheat oven to 350°F. Line bottoms of two 9-inch round cake pans with parchment paper; lightly grease paper. Combine flour, baking powder and salt in medium bowl.

3 Attach flat beater to stand mixer. Beat sugar and butter in mixer bowl on medium-high speed 3 to 5 minutes or until light and fluffy. Add egg whites, two at a time, beating well after each addition. Add vanilla; beat until blended. Add flour mixture alternately with milk, beating well on low speed after each addition. Spread batter evenly in prepared pans.

4 Bake 22 to 25 minutes or until toothpick inserted into centers comes out clean. Cool in pans on wire rack 10 minutes. Loosen edges and invert onto wire rack to cool completely.

5 Prepare Buttercream Frosting and Strawberry Filling. Split cake layers and fill with Lemon Curd. Spread filling over top of one filled cake layer; top with second filled cake layer. Frost top and side of cake with frosting; garnish with fresh strawberries. Store leftovers in refrigerator.

Buttercream Frosting

½ cup (1 stick) butter, softened

3 cups powdered sugar

2 tablespoons milk

½ teaspoon vanilla

Pinch salt

1 Attach flat beater to stand mixer. Beat butter in mixer bowl on medium-high speed until creamy. Add half of powdered sugar; beat on medium-low speed until well blended.

2 Beat in milk, vanilla and salt until blended. Add remaining powdered sugar; beat on medium-high speed 3 to 5 minutes or until light and fluffy.

Strawberry Filling

½ cup Buttercream Frosting (page 136)

¼ cup strawberry jam

¼ cup sliced fresh strawberries

Combine frosting, jam and strawberries in small bowl; mix well.

Chocolate Espresso Cake

Makes 12 servings

2 cups cake flour

1½ teaspoons baking soda

½ teaspoon salt

½ cup (1 stick) butter, softened

1 cup granulated sugar

1 cup packed brown sugar

3 eggs

4 ounces unsweetened chocolate, melted

¾ cup sour cream

1 teaspoon vanilla

1 cup brewed espresso*

Espresso Chocolate Frosting (recipe follows)

*Use fresh brewed espresso, instant espresso powder prepared according to directions on jar or 1 tablespoon instant coffee powder dissolved in 1 cup hot water.

1 Preheat oven to 350°F. Line bottoms of two 9-inch round cake pans with parchment paper; lightly grease paper. Combine flour, baking soda and salt in medium bowl.

2 Attach flat beater to stand mixer. Beat butter and sugars in mixer bowl on medium-high speed until light and fluffy. Add eggs, one at a time, beating well after each addition. Add melted chocolate, sour cream and vanilla; beat until blended. Add flour mixture alternately with espresso, beating well after each addition. Pour batter evenly into prepared pans.

3 Bake 35 minutes or until toothpick inserted into center comes out clean. Cool in pans on wire rack 10 minutes. Loosen edges and invert layers onto wire rack to cool completely.

4 Prepare Espresso Chocolate Frosting. Place one layer on cake plate; frost top. Place second layer over frosting. Frost top and side of cake with frosting.

Espresso Chocolate Frosting

½ cup (1 stick) butter, softened

4 cups powdered sugar

5 to 6 tablespoons brewed espresso, divided

3 ounces semisweet chocolate, melted

1 teaspoon vanilla

Dash of salt

1 Attach flat beater to stand mixer. Beat butter in mixer bowl on medium-high speed 1 minute or until creamy. Gradually add powdered sugar on medium-low speed; beat 2 minutes or until creamy. Add 4 tablespoons espresso; beat until smooth.

2 Add melted chocolate, vanilla and salt. Beat on medium-high speed 3 to 5 minutes or until fluffy, adding remaining espresso, 1 tablespoon at a time, if needed for desired consistency.

Classic Chocolate Cake

Makes about 16 servings

2 cups all-purpose flour

⅔ cup unsweetened cocoa powder

1¼ teaspoons baking soda

1 teaspoon salt

¼ teaspoon baking powder

1 cup granulated sugar

¾ cup (1½ sticks) butter, softened

⅔ cup packed brown sugar

3 eggs

1 teaspoon vanilla

1⅓ cups water

Creamy Chocolate Frosting (page 148)

1 Preheat oven to 350°F. Grease 13×9-inch baking pan. Combine flour, cocoa, baking soda, salt and baking powder in medium bowl.

2 Attach flat beater to stand mixer. Beat granulated sugar, butter and brown sugar in mixer bowl on medium-high speed 2 minutes or until light and fluffy. Add eggs and vanilla; beat 2 minutes. Add flour mixture alternately with water on low speed, beating on low speed after each addition just until blended. Spread batter in prepared pan.

3 Bake 25 to 35 minutes or until toothpick inserted into center comes out clean. Cool completely in pan on wire rack.

4 Prepare Creamy Chocolate Frosting; spread over cooled cake.

Zesty Orange Pound Cake

Makes 12 servings

2 cups all-purpose flour

1 teaspoon baking powder

½ teaspoon salt

1½ cups sugar

1 cup (2 sticks) butter, softened

4 eggs

Grated peel of 2 oranges

3 tablespoons milk

1 tablespoon orange juice

1 Preheat oven to 350°F. Grease 9×5-inch loaf pan. Combine flour, baking powder and salt in medium bowl.

2 Attach flat beater to stand mixer. Beat sugar and butter in mixer bowl on medium-high speed until light and fluffy. Add eggs, one at a time, beating well after each addition. Beat in orange peel, milk and juice. Add flour mixture; mix on low speed just until blended. Spread batter in prepared pan.

3 Bake 1 hour or until toothpick inserted into center comes out clean. Cool in pan on wire rack 10 minutes. Remove to wire rack; cool completely.

Apricot Nectar Cake

Makes 16 servings

4 cups all-purpose flour

1 teaspoon baking powder

¾ teaspoon baking soda

¾ teaspoon salt

2 cups apricot nectar, divided

¾ cup buttermilk

1 cup (2 sticks) butter, softened

2½ cups sugar, divided

4 eggs

Grated peel of 1 lemon

Juice of 1 lemon (about 3 tablespoons)

1 Preheat oven to 325°F. Grease and flour 12-cup bundt pan. Combine flour, baking powder, baking soda and salt in medium bowl. Combine 1½ cups nectar and buttermilk in small bowl.

2 Attach flat beater to stand mixer. Beat butter in mixer bowl on medium speed until smooth. Beat in 2 cups sugar until blended. Add eggs, one at a time, beating well after each addition. Add flour mixture alternately with nectar mixture, mixing on low speed after each addition. Stir in lemon peel. Pour batter into prepared pan.

3 Bake 1 hour or until cake springs back when lightly touched and toothpick inserted near center comes out clean. Cool in pan on wire rack 15 minutes.

4 Meanwhile, combine remaining ½ cup sugar, ½ cup nectar and lemon juice in small saucepan. Bring to a boil over medium-low heat. Boil 1 minute; remove from heat.

5 Invert cake onto serving plate. Poke holes over top of cake and part way down sides with toothpick. Brush top and sides of cake with syrup, allowing it to soak into cake. Cool completely.

NOTE

This cake is better the day after it is made.

Apple-Pear Praline Pie

Makes 8 servings

Double-Crust Pie Pastry (recipe follows)

3 pounds Granny Smith apples, peeled, cored and quartered

1½ pounds pears, peeled, cored and quartered

¾ cup granulated sugar

¼ cup plus 1 tablespoon all-purpose flour, divided

4 teaspoons ground cinnamon

¼ teaspoon salt

½ cup (1 stick) plus 2 tablespoons butter, divided

1 cup packed brown sugar

1 tablespoon half-and-half

1 cup chopped pecans

1 Prepare Double-Crust Pie Pastry.

2 Assemble Rotor Slicer/Shredder with thick slicing cone; attach to stand mixer. Slice apples and pears into mixer bowl. Stir in granulated sugar, ¼ cup flour, cinnamon and salt; toss to coat. Let stand 15 minutes.

3 Preheat oven to 350°F. Roll half of pastry into 11-inch circle on floured surface. Line deep-dish 9-inch pie plate with pastry; sprinkle with remaining 1 tablespoon flour. Spoon fruit mixture into crust; dot with 2 tablespoons butter. Roll out remaining pastry into 10-inch circle. Place over filling; seal and flute edge. Cut slits in top crust to vent. Bake 1 hour.

4 Combine remaining ½ cup butter, brown sugar and half-and-half in small saucepan; bring to a boil over medium heat, stirring frequently. Boil 2 minutes, stirring constantly. Remove from heat; stir in pecans. Let stand until thickened to spreadable consistency. Spread over pie. Serve warm or at room temperature.

Double-Crust Pie Pastry

2½ cups all-purpose flour

1 teaspoon salt

1 teaspoon sugar

1 cup (2 sticks) cold butter, cubed

7 tablespoons ice water

1 tablespoon cider vinegar

1 Attach flat beater to stand mixer. Combine flour, salt and sugar in mixer bowl. Add butter; mix on low speed 1 minute or until coarse crumbs form. Combine ice water and vinegar in small bowl.

2 With mixer running on low speed, drizzle in enough water mixture just until dough starts to come together. Turn out dough onto lightly floured surface; press into a ball. Divide in half. Shape each half into a disc; wrap in plastic wrap. Refrigerate 30 minutes.

Carrot Cake

Makes 12 servings

1 pound carrots, peeled and trimmed

2½ cups all-purpose flour

2 tablespoons ground cinnamon, divided

1 teaspoon salt

1 teaspoon baking soda

½ teaspoon ground ginger

2 cups granulated sugar

1½ cups vegetable oil

1 teaspoon vanilla

4 eggs, beaten

1 cup canned crushed pineapple, drained and juice reserved

¾ cup chopped pecans

½ cup golden raisins

Additional pineapple juice

Cream Cheese Frosting (recipe follows)

1 Preheat oven to 350°F. Grease and flour two 8-inch round cake pans. Assemble Food Processor attachment with shredding disc; attach to stand mixer. Shred carrots into large bowl.

2 Sift flour, 1 tablespoon cinnamon, salt, baking soda and ginger into medium bowl.

3 Remove Food Processor; attach flat beater. Beat granulated sugar, oil and vanilla in mixer bowl on low speed until blended. Add flour mixture alternately with eggs, mixing well on low speed after each addition. Stir in carrots, pineapple, pecans and raisins until well blended. Spread batter evenly in prepared pans.

4 Bake 45 to 50 minutes or until toothpick inserted into centers comes out clean. Combine reserved pineapple juice with enough additional pineapple juice to equal 2 cups. Poke holes in warm cake with wooden skewer; pour 1 cup juice over each cake. Let stand in pans until cool and juice is absorbed.

5 Prepare Cream Cheese Frosting. Invert one cake layer onto serving plate; spread about 1 cup frosting over cake. Top with second cake layer; frost top and side of cake. Sprinkle with remaining 1 tablespoon cinnamon. Store in refrigerator.

Cream Cheese Frosting

- 1 package (8 ounces) cream cheese, softened
- ½ cup (1 stick) butter, softened
- 2 tablespoons vanilla
- 2 cups powdered sugar
- 3 to 5 tablespoons milk

1 Attach flat beater to stand mixer. Beat cream cheese, butter and vanilla in mixer bowl on medium speed 2 minutes or until light and fluffy.

2 Beat in powdered sugar on low speed until well blended. Beat on medium speed 3 minutes or until fluffy. If frosting is too thick, add milk, 1 tablespoon at a time, until desired consistency is reached.

Old-Fashioned Devil's Food Cake

Makes 12 servings

2 cups cake flour

½ cup unsweetened cocoa powder

2 teaspoons baking powder

½ teaspoon baking soda

½ teaspoon salt

6 tablespoons butter, softened

1½ cups granulated sugar

3 eggs

1½ teaspoons vanilla

1 cup buttermilk*

Creamy Chocolate Frosting (recipe follows)

Or substitute 1 tablespoon vinegar or lemon juice and enough milk to equal 1 cup. Let stand 5 minutes.

1 Preheat oven to 350°F. Grease and flour three 8-inch round cake pans. Combine flour, cocoa, baking powder, baking soda and salt in medium bowl.

2 Attach flat beater to stand mixer. Beat butter and granulated sugar in mixer bowl on medium speed until fluffy. Beat in eggs and vanilla. Add flour mixture alternately with buttermilk, beating well on low speed after each addition. Spread batter evenly in prepared pans.

3 Bake 25 to 30 minutes or until toothpick inserted into centers comes out clean. Cool in pans on wire racks 10 minutes. Remove from pans to wire racks; cool completely.

4 Meanwhile, prepare Creamy Chocolate Frosting.

5 Place one cake layer on serving plate; spread with frosting. Repeat with remaining two cake layers and frosting. Frost top and side of cake.

Creamy Chocolate Frosting

6 tablespoons butter, softened

5 cups powdered sugar

½ cup unsweetened cocoa powder

6 tablespoons milk

1 teaspoon vanilla

1 Attach flat beater to stand mixer. Beat butter in mixer bowl on medium speed 2 minutes or until creamy. Gradually add powdered sugar and cocoa, beating until smooth.

2 Add milk, 1 tablespoon at a time, and vanilla until desired consistency is reached. Beat 2 minutes on medium-high speed until fluffy.

White Chocolate Cake

Makes 12 servings

2 cups all-purpose flour

2¼ teaspoons baking powder

½ teaspoon salt

1 cup milk

½ cup (1 stick) butter

4 ounces white chocolate, broken into pieces

1½ cups sugar

4 eggs

1 teaspoon vanilla

12 ounces bittersweet chocolate, chopped

1¼ cups whipping cream

White chocolate curls (optional)

1 Preheat oven to 350°F. Grease two 9-inch round cake pans. Combine flour, baking powder and salt in medium bowl.

2 Combine milk, butter and white chocolate in medium saucepan; cook and stir over medium-low heat until melted and smooth.

3 Attach flat beater to stand mixer. Beat sugar and eggs in mixer bowl on medium speed 3 minutes or until pale and thick. Add vanilla; beat until blended. Gradually add flour mixture, beating on low speed until well blended. Gradually beat in milk mixture. Spread batter in prepared pans.

4 Bake 24 to 28 minutes or until toothpick inserted into centers comes out clean. Cool in pans 15 minutes. Remove to wire racks; cool completely.

5 For ganache, place bittersweet chocolate in medium bowl. Heat cream in small saucepan over medium-low heat until bubbles appear around edge of pan. Pour over chocolate; let stand 2 minutes. Stir until smooth. Let stand 15 minutes or until thick enough to spread.

6 Place one cake layer on serving plate; spread with one third of ganache. Top with remaining cake layer; frost top and side of cake with remaining ganache. Garnish with white chocolate curls.

TIP
For a perfectly smooth surface, the ganache may need to be reheated slightly until pourable.

Angel Food Cake

Makes 12 servings

1¼ cups cake flour

1⅓ cups plus ½ cup sugar, divided

12 egg whites

1½ teaspoons vanilla

1¼ teaspoons cream of tartar

¼ teaspoon salt (optional)

Fresh strawberries (optional)

1 Preheat oven to 350°F. Sift together flour and ½ cup sugar two times into medium bowl.

2 Attach wire whip to stand mixer. Whip egg whites, vanilla, cream of tartar and salt, if desired, in mixer bowl on high speed until soft peaks form.

3 Gradually add remaining 1⅓ cups sugar, beating well until stiff peaks form. Fold in flour mixture. Pour into *ungreased* 10-inch tube pan.

4 Bake 35 to 40 minutes or until cake springs back when lightly touched.

5 Invert pan; place on top of clean empty bottle. Cool completely in pan. Serve with strawberries, if desired.

Flourless Chocolate Cake

Makes 12 servings

4 ounces unsweetened chocolate, coarsely chopped

4 ounces semisweet chocolate, coarsely chopped

½ cup heavy cream

3 eggs, at room temperature

½ cup sugar

¼ cup strong brewed coffee

¼ teaspoon salt

½ cup chopped walnuts, divided

Sweetened Whipped Cream (page 5, optional)

1 Preheat oven to 350°F. Grease 8-inch round cake pan.

2 Place unsweetened chocolate, semisweet chocolate and cream in medium heavy saucepan; cook over very low heat, stirring constantly until melted and smooth.

3 Attach flat beater to stand mixer. Beat eggs and sugar in mixer bowl on high speed about 7 minutes or until pale and thick. Add chocolate mixture, coffee and salt to egg mixture; beat on medium speed 1 to 2 minutes or until well blended. Stir in ¼ cup walnuts.

4 Spread in prepared pan; sprinkle with remaining ¼ cup walnuts. Place pan in large baking pan; add enough hot water to baking pan to reach halfway up side of cake pan.

5 Bake 30 to 35 minutes or until set but still soft in center. Loosen edge of cake with knife; place serving plate upside down over pan and invert. Prepare Sweetened Whipped Cream, if desired. Serve with warm cake.

Coconut Spice Cake

Makes 12 servings

½ cup granulated sugar, plus additional for pans

2½ cups all-purpose flour

1½ teaspoons baking powder

¾ teaspoon baking soda

½ teaspoon salt

1½ teaspoons ground cinnamon

¼ teaspoon ground nutmeg

¼ teaspoon ground allspice

¼ teaspoon ground cardamom

1½ cups milk or half-and-half

¼ cup molasses

½ cup (1 stick) butter, softened

½ cup packed brown sugar

4 eggs

1 teaspoon vanilla

1½ cups shredded coconut

Creamy Orange Frosting (recipe follows)

Candied Orange Rose (recipe follows, optional)

⅔ cup orange marmalade

1 Preheat oven to 350°F. Grease three 8-inch round cake pans. Line bottoms with parchment paper; grease paper. Sprinkle with enough granulated sugar to lightly coat bottoms and sides of pans. Combine flour, baking powder, baking soda, salt and spices in medium bowl. Combine milk and molasses in 2-cup measuring cup.

2 Attach flat beater to stand mixer. Beat butter in mixer bowl on medium speed until creamy. Add ½ cup granulated sugar and brown sugar; beat on medium-high speed until light and fluffy. Add eggs, one at a time, beating well after each addition. Beat in vanilla. Add flour mixture alternately with milk mixture, beating well on low speed after each addition. Stir in coconut. Spread evenly in prepared pans.

3 Bake 20 to 23 minutes or until toothpick inserted into centers comes out clean. Cool in pans on wire racks 10 minutes. Loosen edges; turn out onto wire racks and peel off parchment paper. Cool completely.

4 Prepare Creamy Orange Frosting and Candied Orange Rose, if desired.

5 Spread marmalade over two cake layers; stack on serving plate. Top with third cake layer. Frost with Creamy Orange Frosting and garnish with candied orange. Store in refrigerator.

Creamy Orange Frosting

3 ounces cream cheese, softened

2 cups powdered sugar

1 teaspoon grated orange peel

4 to 6 teaspoons fresh orange juice

1 Attach flat beater to stand mixer. Beat cream cheese in mixer bowl on medium-high speed until creamy.

2 Gradually add powdered sugar on low speed, beating until fluffy. Blend in orange peel and juice, 1 teaspoon at a time, if necessary to reach desired consistency.

Candied Orange Rose

1 cup granulated sugar

1 cup water

1 orange

1 Combine sugar and water in medium saucepan. Bring to a boil over medium-high heat, stirring occasionally.

2 Meanwhile, thinly peel orange with sharp knife, leaving as much membrane on orange as possible. Carefully roll up peel, starting at one short end; secure with toothpick. Place on slotted spoon; add to sugar syrup.

3 Reduce heat to low; simmer 5 to 10 minutes or until orange rind turns translucent. Remove from syrup with slotted spoon; cool on waxed paper-covered plate. Remove toothpick.

Spiced Peach Pie

Makes 8 servings

Double-Crust Pie Pastry
(page 144)

2 pounds fresh peaches,
   peeled *or* 5 cups frozen
   sliced peaches, thawed
   and well drained

1 egg, separated

1 cup sugar

2 tablespoons cornstarch

2 teaspoons ground
   cinnamon

½ teaspoon ground nutmeg

⅛ teaspoon salt

½ cup fresh orange juice

1 teaspoon vanilla

1 tablespoon butter, cut
   into small pieces

1 teaspoon cold water

1 Prepare Double-Crust Pie Pastry.

2 Preheat oven to 400°F.

3 Roll out half of pastry on floured surface into 11-inch circle.
  Line 9-inch pie plate with pastry. Attach wire whip to stand
  mixer. Whip egg white in mixer bowl until frothy. Brush
  over pastry.

4 Combine sugar, cornstarch, cinnamon, nutmeg and salt in
  large bowl; mix well. Stir in orange juice and vanilla. Add
  peaches; toss lightly to coat. Spoon into crust; dot with
  butter.

5 Roll out remaining pastry into 10-inch circle. Cut into ½-inch-
  wide strips. Arrange in lattice design over peaches. Tuck strips
  under and flute edge. Whisk egg yolk and water in small
  bowl; brush over pastry.

6 Bake 50 minutes or until pastry is golden brown and filling is
  thick and bubbly. Cover loosely with foil after 30 minutes to
  prevent overbrowning, if necessary. Cool on wire rack. Serve
  warm or at room temperature. Refrigerate leftovers.

CHAPTER 9
DESSERTS

Black and White Sandwich Cookies

Makes 22 to 24 cookies

COOKIES

- 1¼ cups (2½ sticks) butter
- ¾ cup granulated sugar
- 1 egg
- 1½ teaspoons vanilla
- 2⅓ cups all-purpose flour, divided
- ¼ teaspoon salt
- ⅓ cup unsweetened cocoa powder

FILLING

- 4 ounces cream cheese
- ½ cup (1 stick) butter
- 2 cups plus 2 tablespoons powdered sugar
- 2 tablespoons unsweetened cocoa powder

1 For cookies, attach flat beater to stand mixer. Beat 1¼ cups butter and granulated sugar in mixer bowl on medium-high speed until creamy. Beat in egg and vanilla until well blended. Beat in 2 cups flour and salt on low speed until combined.

2 Remove half of dough to medium bowl; stir in remaining ⅓ cup flour. Add ⅓ cup cocoa to dough in mixer bowl; beat just until blended. Wrap doughs separately in plastic wrap; refrigerate 30 minutes or until firm.

3 Preheat oven to 350°F. Line cookie sheets with parchment paper. Roll out plain dough on floured surface to ¼-inch thickness. Cut out 2-inch circles; place 2 inches apart on prepared cookie sheets. Repeat with chocolate dough.

4 Bake 8 to 10 minutes or until set but not browned. Remove to wire racks; cool completely.

5 For filling, attach flat beater to stand mixer. Beat ½ cup butter and cream cheese in mixer bowl on medium speed until well blended. Add 2 cups powdered sugar; beat until creamy. Remove half of filling to small bowl; stir in remaining 2 tablespoons powdered sugar. Add 2 tablespoons cocoa to filling in mixer bowl; beat until smooth.

6 Pipe or spread chocolate frosting on flat side of half of plain cookies; top with remaining plain cookies. Pipe or spread vanilla frosting on flat side of half of chocolate cookies; top with remaining chocolate cookies.

Vanilla Biscuits with Strawberries and Whipped Cream

Makes about 20 servings

2 cups all-purpose flour

3 tablespoons granulated sugar, divided

1 tablespoon baking powder

¼ teaspoon salt

½ cup (1 stick) cold butter, cut into pieces

¾ cup buttermilk

2 teaspoons vanilla

1½ pounds fresh strawberries, hulled

2 cups (1 pint) heavy cream

3 tablespoons powdered sugar

½ teaspoon grated lemon peel

1 Preheat oven to 425°F. Line baking sheet with parchment paper.

2 Attach flat beater to stand mixer. Combine flour, 2 tablespoons granulated sugar, baking powder and salt in mixer bowl; mix on low speed 10 seconds or until blended. Add butter; mix on low speed 1 to 2 minutes or until mixture resembles coarse crumbs. With mixer running on low speed, add buttermilk and vanilla. Mix just until rough dough forms.

3 Turn out dough onto lightly floured surface; gather into a ball. Roll or pat dough to ½-inch thickness. Cut circles with 3-inch biscuit cutter; place on prepared baking sheet.

4 Bake 10 to 15 minutes or until lightly browned. Remove to wire rack; cool completely.

5 Assemble Food Processor attachment with adjustable slicing disc; attach to stand mixer. Slide to third notch for medium slices. Slice strawberries horizontally into large bowl. Stir in remaining 1 tablespoon granulated sugar.

6 Remove Food Processor; attach wire whip. Combine cream and powdered sugar in clean mixer bowl; whip on high speed 3 minutes or until stiff peaks form. Mix in lemon peel.

7 Slice biscuits in half. Fill with whipped cream and strawberry slices; garnish with additional whipped cream and strawberry slices.

Cinnamon Honey Ice Cream

2 cups milk

¾ cup honey

1 teaspoon ground cinnamon

Pinch salt

2 eggs, beaten

2 cups heavy cream

2 teaspoons vanilla

Makes about 1 quart ice cream

1 Bring milk to a simmer in medium saucepan over medium heat. *Do not boil.* Stir in honey, cinnamon and salt.

2 Slowly whisk ½ cup hot milk mixture into eggs; whisk egg mixture into saucepan. Cook over medium-low heat 5 minutes or until mixture thickens slightly, stirring frequently.

3 Cool to room temperature. Stir in cream and vanilla. Cover and refrigerate 2 hours or until cold.

4 Attach frozen Ice Cream Maker bowl and dasher to stand mixer. Turn mixer to stir; pour cold mixture into bowl with mixer running. Continue to stir 20 to 30 minutes or until consistency of soft-serve ice cream.

5 Transfer ice cream to airtight container; freeze several hours until firm.

Fresh Fruit Tart

Makes 8 to 10 servings

¾ cup (1½ sticks) plus 1 tablespoon butter, softened, divided

⅔ cup sugar, divided

1 teaspoon grated lemon peel

3 teaspoons vanilla, divided

1¾ cups all-purpose flour

¼ teaspoon salt

3 egg yolks

1½ tablespoons cornstarch

1 cup plus 1 tablespoon half-and-half, divided

½ firm ripe banana

3 fresh strawberries, hulled

1 firm ripe kiwi, peeled

1 peach or nectarine, pitted and halved

½ mango, peeled and pitted

¼ cup *each* raspberries, blueberries and blackberries

1 Preheat oven to 350°F.

2 Attach flat beater to stand mixer. Beat ¾ cup butter, ⅓ cup sugar and lemon peel in mixer bowl on medium-high speed about 1 minute or until well blended. Mix in 2 teaspoons vanilla until blended. Add flour and salt; mix on low speed about 1 minute or until fine crumbs form. Turn out dough onto lightly floured surface; gather into a ball. Press dough into 9- or 10-inch tart pan with removable bottom; cover with parchment paper and fill with dried beans or rice. Bake 20 minutes. Remove beans and parchment; prick bottom of crust all over with fork. Bake 10 to 15 minutes or until lightly browned. Cool completely.

3 Combine egg yolks and remaining ⅓ cup sugar in clean mixer bowl; beat on medium speed 2 to 3 minutes or until mixture is pale and slightly thickened. Beat in cornstarch and remaining 1 teaspoon vanilla on low speed until well blended.

4 Bring 1 cup half-and-half to a boil in medium saucepan. With mixer running on low speed, pour hot half-and-half into egg mixture in thin steady stream. Pour mixture into same saucepan. Cook over medium heat 3 to 5 minutes or until mixture thickens, whisking constantly. Remove from heat; whisk in remaining 1 tablespoon half-and-half and 1 tablespoon butter. Press through fine mesh sieve into medium bowl; cool slightly. Press plastic wrap directly onto surface; refrigerate until cold.

5 Assemble Food Processor attachment with adjustable slicing disc; attach to stand mixer. Slide to third notch; slice banana and strawberries into large bowl. Slide to fourth notch; slice kiwi, peach and mango. Spread filling over crust; top with sliced fruit and berries.

Butter Almond Ice Cream with Amaretto Caramel Sauce

Makes about 1½ quarts ice cream

ICE CREAM

¼ cup (½ stick) butter

1¼ cups (about 5 ounces) sliced natural almonds

3 cups half-and-half

6 egg yolks

1 cup sugar

¾ teaspoon almond extract

½ teaspoon vanilla

SAUCE

1 cup sugar

¼ cup water

1 cup heavy cream, heated

2 tablespoons butter, thinly sliced

2 tablespoons amaretto *or* ½ teaspoon almond extract

Pinch of salt

1 For ice cream, melt butter in small heavy saucepan over medium heat. Bring to a boil and cook 3 minutes or until butter turns light brown. Pour brown butter into small bowl, leaving any browned specks in saucepan.

2 Preheat oven to 350°F. Spread almonds on baking sheet. Bake 10 minutes or until almonds are fragrant and lightly browned, stirring occasionally. Drizzle 2 tablespoons melted brown butter over almonds and toss to coat. Let cool.

3 Attach wire whip to stand mixer. Combine half-and-half and remaining brown butter in medium saucepan; bring to simmer over medium heat, stirring frequently. Remove from heat. Whip yolks and sugar in mixer bowl on medium speed 1 minute or until pale and thickened. Gradually whisk in hot half-and-half. Pour mixture into saucepan and cook over medium-low heat, stirring constantly with wooden spoon, until custard lightly coats spoon and instant-read thermometer reads 185°F. Immediately pour custard through fine-mesh sieve into medium bowl. Stir in almond extract and vanilla. Refrigerate several hours or until cold.

4 Remove wire whip. Attach frozen Ice Cream Maker bowl and dasher to stand mixer. Turn mixer to stir; pour cold mixture into bowl with mixer running. Continue to stir 20 to 30 minutes or until consistency of soft-serve ice cream. Stir in 1 cup almonds during last 2 minutes of mixing.

5 Transfer ice cream to airtight container; freeze several hours until firm.

6 For sauce, combine sugar and water in heavy medium saucepan. Cook over medium-high heat, stirring until sugar dissolves. Cook without stirring 3 to 5 minutes or until caramel is copper colored and smoking, brushing down

crystals that form on inside of pan with pastry brush dipped in cold water and swirling pan occasionally. Remove from heat. Gradually stir in heavy cream (sauce will boil up) until caramel dissolves. Add butter; stir over medium heat until melted. Stir in amaretto and salt. Let cool to room temperature.

7 Serve ice cream topped with sauce and remaining almonds.

Pots de Crème au Chocolat

Makes 6 servings

2 cups heavy cream

1 tablespoon sugar

4 ounces semisweet chocolate, finely chopped

5 egg yolks

Sweetened Whipped Cream (page 5, optional)

1 Preheat oven to 325°F. Heat cream and sugar in medium heavy saucepan over medium heat until sugar is dissolved, stirring constantly. Reduce heat to low; stir in chocolate until melted and smooth. Remove from heat.

2 Attach wire whip to stand mixer. Whip egg yolks in mixer bowl on medium-high speed 1 minute. Gradually add chocolate mixture on low speed, whipping until well blended.

3 Pour mixture evenly into six 6-ounce custard cups or crème pots. Place cups in 13×9-inch baking pan; fill pan with boiling water halfway up sides of cups.

4 Bake 20 to 25 minutes or until firm. Cool to room temperature. Refrigerate at least 2 hours. Prepare Sweetened Whipped Cream, if desired. Serve with pots de crème.

Rosemary-Honey Shortbread Cookies

Makes 2 dozen cookies

2 cups all-purpose flour

1 tablespoon fresh
   rosemary leaves,*
   minced

½ teaspoon salt

½ teaspoon baking powder

¾ cup (1½ sticks) butter,
   softened

½ cup powdered sugar

2 tablespoons honey

*For best flavor, use only fresh rosemary
or substitute fresh or dried lavender
buds.*

1 Combine flour, rosemary, salt and baking powder in medium bowl.

2 Attach flat beater to stand mixer. Beat butter, powdered sugar and honey in mixer bowl on medium speed until creamy. Beat in flour mixture just until blended. (Mixture will be crumbly.)

3 Shape dough into log. Wrap in plastic wrap; refrigerate 1 hour or until firm. (Dough can be refrigerated several days.)

4 Preheat oven to 350°F. Line cookie sheets with parchment paper. Cut log into ½-inch slices. Place 2 inches apart on prepared cookie sheets. Bake 10 to 13 minutes or until set. Cool on cookie sheets 1 minute. Remove to wire racks; cool completely.

Pineapple-Ginger Sherbet

Makes about 1½ quarts sherbet

2 cans (8 ounces each) crushed pineapple in juice

¾ cup granulated sugar, divided

1 envelope unflavored gelatin

¼ cup fresh orange juice

2 tablespoons honey

1 tablespoon grated fresh ginger

1½ teaspoons vanilla

2 cups buttermilk

1 Drain one can of pineapple, reserving juice.

2 Combine ¼ cup sugar and gelatin in small saucepan. Add reserved pineapple juice and orange juice. Cook over low heat until gelatin dissolves, stirring constantly. Remove from heat.

3 Combine drained pineapple, undrained pineapple, remaining ½ cup sugar, honey, ginger and vanilla in food processor. Cover and process until smooth. Add gelatin mixture; process until combined. Stir in buttermilk.

4 Attach frozen Ice Cream Maker bowl and dasher to stand mixer. Turn mixer to stir; pour cold mixture into bowl with mixer running. Continue to stir 20 to 30 minutes or until consistency of soft-serve ice cream.

5 Transfer sherbet to airtight container; freeze several hours until firm.

Pear Caramel Sauce

Makes ¾ cup sauce

2 to 3 Comice or Anjou
    pears, quartered

½ cup sugar

2 tablespoons water

Pinch cream of tartar

2 tablespoons heavy cream

1 tablespoon butter

⅛ teaspoon salt

1 tablespoon pear-flavored
    vodka or liqueur

1 Assemble Juicer and Sauce attachment with low pulp screen; attach to stand mixer. Juice pears. Strain juice through fine-mesh sieve. Measure 1 cup juice.

2 Pour juice into small saucepan. Cook over medium-high heat about 10 minutes or until thickened and reduced to ¼ cup, stirring occasionally. Set aside to cool.

3 Combine sugar, 2 tablespoons water and cream of tartar in medium saucepan. Bring to a boil over medium heat, stirring until sugar dissolves. When mixture starts to boil, cover pan for 2 minutes (steam will dissolve sugar crystals on side of pan). Remove cover; cook without stirring 8 to 10 minutes or until mixture is light amber in color, swirling pan occasionally.

4 Remove heat; carefully whisk in reduced pear juice, cream, butter and salt until smooth (mixture will bubble vigorously). Stir in vodka; cool completely. Store in airtight jar or container in the refrigerator up to 2 weeks.

Espresso Gelato

+

Makes about 1½ quarts gelato

2½ cups whole milk

1 cup heavy cream

¾ cup very coarsely ground espresso or Italian roast coffee beans

1 cup sugar

3 egg yolks

1 tablespoon plus 2 teaspoons cornstarch

1 teaspoon vanilla

1 cup mini chocolate chips (optional)

1 Heat milk, cream and espresso beans in medium heavy saucepan over medium heat until bubbles form around edge of pan. Remove from heat; let steep for 10 minutes.

2 Attach wire whip to stand mixer. Whip sugar, egg yolks and cornstarch in mixer bowl on medium speed. With mixer running on medium speed, pour hot cream mixture into sugar mixture in thin steady stream. Rinse saucepan. Pour cream mixture into saucepan. Cook over medium heat until mixture is barely simmering, whisking constantly. Strain through fine-mesh sieve into medium bowl. Stir in vanilla. Refrigerate at least 2 hours or until cold.

3 Attach frozen Ice Cream Maker bowl and dasher to stand mixer. Turn mixer to stir; pour cold mixture into bowl with mixer running. Continue to stir 20 to 30 minutes or until consistency of soft-serve ice cream. Stir in chocolate chips during last 2 minutes of mixing, if desired.

4 Transfer ice cream to airtight container; freeze several hours until firm.

Choco-Orange Macadamia Cookies

Makes about 3 dozen cookies

1 cup macadamia nuts

2 cups plus 1 tablespoon all-purpose flour

½ teaspoon baking powder

½ teaspoon salt

¾ cup (1½ sticks) butter, melted and cooled

1 cup packed brown sugar

6 tablespoons granulated sugar

2 teaspoons grated orange peel

2 teaspoons vanilla

1 whole egg

1 egg yolk

1 cup semisweet chocolate chips

½ cup flaked coconut

1 Preheat oven to 350°F.

2 Place macadamia nuts in shallow baking pan. Bake 8 to 10 minutes or until golden brown and fragrant, stirring occasionally. (Nuts burn easily so watch carefully.) Cool completely. Coarsely chop nuts; set aside.

3 Combine flour, baking powder and salt in medium bowl. Attach flat beater to stand mixer. Beat butter, sugars, orange peel and vanilla in mixer bowl on medium-high speed until light and fluffy. Beat in whole egg and egg yolk until blended. Gradually add flour mixture, beating on low speed until blended. Stir in nuts, chocolate chips and coconut.

4 Drop dough by rounded tablespoonfuls 2 inches apart onto ungreased cookie sheets.

5 Bake 10 to 12 minutes or until edges are lightly browned and centers are almost set. Cool on cookie sheets 1 minute. Remove to wire racks; cool completely.

Fresh Corn Ice Cream

Makes 1½ pints ice cream

1 medium ear corn

1 cup whole milk, plus more if necessary

2 cups half-and-half

¼ cup granulated sugar

¼ cup packed brown sugar

2 egg yolks

¼ teaspoon vanilla

¾ cup chopped salted pecans

1 Scrape kernels from cob into medium heavy saucepan; add cob. Pour in 1 cup milk. Partially cover and cook over very low heat 30 minutes. (If milk evaporates completely, add ¼ cup more.) Discard corncob.

2 Stir half-and-half and sugars into corn mixture. Cook, uncovered, over low heat until sugar dissolves and liquid comes to a simmer, stirring frequently.

3 Whisk egg yolks in small bowl. Gradually whisk in ½ cup corn mixture; slowly whisk mixture into saucepan. Cook over medium heat 10 minutes or until slightly thickened, stirring frequently. Remove from heat. Stir in vanilla. Pour into medium bowl. Refrigerate at least 2 hours or until completely cold.

4 Attach frozen Ice Cream Maker bowl and dasher to stand mixer. Turn mixer to stir; pour cold mixture into bowl with mixer running. Continue to stir 20 to 30 minutes or until consistency of soft-serve ice cream. Add pecans during last minute of stirring.

5 Transfer ice cream to airtight container; freeze several hours until firm.

Crème Brûlée

Makes 6 servings

2 cups heavy cream

4 egg yolks

¼ cup plus 2 tablespoons sugar, divided

1 teaspoon vanilla

1 Preheat oven to 300°F. Heat cream in medium heavy saucepan over medium-low heat until small bubbles appear around edge of pan (130° to 140°F).

2 Attach wire whip to stand mixer. Whisk egg yolks and ¼ cup sugar in mixer bowl on medium-high speed until well blended. Gradually whisk in cream on low speed until blended. Stir in vanilla. Pour mixture into six small shallow baking dishes or 4-ounce custard cups. Place cups in 13×9-inch baking pan; fill pan with boiling water halfway up sides of dishes.

3 Bake 25 to 30 minutes for shallow dishes (30 to 35 minutes for custard cups) or until set in center. (Mixture may look thin, but it will set upon cooling.) Cool to room temperature. Refrigerate at least 4 hours or up to 24 hours.

4 Preheat broiler. Sprinkle remaining 2 tablespoons sugar evenly over custards. Broil 6 inches from heat about 30 seconds or until golden crust forms, rotating if necessary to brown sugar evenly. Serve immediately.